THE OPEN CIRCLE

The Meaning of Christian Brotherhood

THE OPEN CIRCLE
The Meaning of Christian Brotherhood

by JOSEPH RATZINGER

translated by W. A. Glen-Doeple

SHEED AND WARD : New York

To Professor Albert Lang
on His Seventieth Birthday

Contents

Introduction by Robert McAfee Brown	9
Foreword	19
Abbreviations	21

AN HISTORICAL ANALYSIS   24

The Idea of Brotherhood before and outside
Christianity   27
  1. "Brother" in Ancient Greece   27
  *2. The Idea of Brotherhood in the Old
     Testament*   28
  3. The Development in Hellenism   35
  4. The Enlightenment and Marxism   39

The Development of the Idea of Brotherhood in
Early Christianity   45
  1. "Brother" in the Words of Christ   45
  *2. The Development within the New
     Testament, Especially in Paul*   56
  3. The Idea of Brotherhood in the Fathers   65

7

The Open Circle

AN ATTEMPT AT SYNTHESIS   69

The Basis of Christian Brotherhood: Faith   73

The Removal of Barriers within the Brotherhood
   of Christians   87

The Limits of the Brotherly Community   97

True Universalism   109

POSTSCRIPT   121

8

Introduction

Perhaps the most initially striking thing about Father Joseph Ratzinger's essay on *Christian Brotherhood* is that its point of origin is both pre-conciliar and pre-Johannine. American Christians, who all too easily assume that creative currents on the Roman Catholic scene are the exclusive result of Pope John and Vatican II, need therefore to be reminded that the material in the following pages is not so much the sort of thing made possible by Vatican II, but, on the contrary, the sort of thing that made Vatican II possible. That the Council has had such an impact on the Christian world is attributable not only to the remarkable breakthrough that occurred during the course of its four sessions, but also to the fact that for many years before the Council a number of Catholic theologians were quietly sowing the seeds that came to harvest in the sixteen documents promulgated in St. Peter's.

Among those whose work bore fruit at the Council,

Fr. Ratzinger's name rates an important place. Not only do some of the ideas in *The Open Circle: the Meaning of Christian Brotherhood* receive authoritative formulation in conciliar documents, but other contributions of Fr. Ratzinger, notably his essay in Rahner and Ratzinger, *The Episcopate and the Primacy* (*Quaestiones Disputatae*, Herder and Herder, 1962, pp. 37–63) likewise foreshadow positions that the Council fathers came to adopt. That at some points (as will be suggested herein) the Council has gone beyond the ideas contained in these pre-conciliar theological reflections is only an indication that the Spirit is not static.

There are few themes more ecumenically important than "Christian brotherhood," few themes more ecumenically difficult, and few themes more susceptible to ecumenical examination across the boundaries of division. (That a Protestant writes the Introduction to this Roman Catholic book is at least a modest symbol of the latter point.) That the path of ecumenical insight is not a one-way street is made even clearer, however, by Fr. Ratzinger's extensive use of materials from the Swiss Reformed theoloigan, Karl Barth, whose treatment of election in *Church Dogmatics* (T. and T. Clark, II/2, pp. 3–506) is a notable breakthrough for fresh Catholic as well as Calvinist reflection.

But grave problems of understanding remain, even

when we begin to read and use one another's insights, and it is to Fr. Ratzinger's credit that from the beginning, and throughout, he indicates very clearly that a concept of brotherhood not only binds men together, but also separates them. His realistic analysis of this point is telling and convincing. Brotherhood creates the problem of the "two zones," that is, the brotherhood I experience in the close bond of a community of shared commitment and conviction, and the brotherhood I am called upon to exemplify in my dealings with all men everywhere. I may belong to both the community of the faithful and the community of the needful, but they are not coterminus, and part of the real problem of "Christian brotherhood" ever since New Testament times has been to find ways of relating them to one another.

The Stoics, together with the philosophers of the Enlightenment, sought to obliterate the barriers between the "two zones" by the creation of one single universal brotherhood. The idea is appealing, even breathtaking, but as Fr. Ratzinger points out, it is bought at a heavy price, for "a brotherhood which embraces everyone equally cannot expect to be taken seriously by anyone." Thus, rather than seeking to obliterate the "two zones," Fr. Ratzinger insists that the acknowledgement of their reality must be the presupposition from which the Christian works to make brotherhood increasingly all-embracing, but without succumbing to unreality or sentimentality.

The question, then, for the Christian, is twofold: 1) What is his relation to the one who stands outside the Christian fellowship itself? 2) What is his relation to the "brother" within a Christian fellowship that has become historically divided? And Fr. Ratzinger's over-all response is surely that the inner ring of brotherhood must not exist for its own sake, becoming ingrown and exotic, but for the sake of the wider ring to which it must continually reach out and with which it must increasingly identify. The separating off, he insists, is for the sake of service to the whole. In some very moving paragraphs, Fr. Ratzinger points out that this means "missionizing," *agape*, and suffering by the Christian community for the sake of all men.

At this point, of course, the Protestant and the Catholic can increasingly make common cause. All Christians share a concern for the world, not as a place to which they go on ecclesiastical scalping expeditions, seeking to bring back tokens of their victories into the safe fortresses of their respective churchly institutions, but rather, as Fr. Ratzinger says, as those who must be willing to serve apart from the assurance of numerical gain, "directing their love to all those who need them, without asking for thanks or a response." And what has happened, since Fr. Ratzinger originally wrote these words, is that Protestants and Catholics have now been empowered to do this *together*, to a far greater degree than could have been anticipated even recently. The Vatican II decree *On Ecumenism* (*cf.* articles 4 and 12), together with portions of the decree *On The Missionary Activity of the Church* (*cf.* articles 7, 11, 15, 35, 41) and the pastoral constitution *On the Church in the World Today* (*cf.* articles 40, 88, 92), give a conciliar charter for common concern that is a most hopeful augury for future common ecumenical outreach in service and love.

In this new situation, Christians can recognize that they represent a minority of mankind and that, as Fr. Karl Rahner has frequently suggested, they will be in *diaspora*, scattered, dispersed, for the foreseeable future (*cf.* Rahner, *The Christian Commitment*, Sheed and Ward, 1963, pp. 3–37). Rather than reacting to this situation in panic, Christians can affirm it joyfully as the situation in which God has placed them today and find ways to serve the wider community comprising all mankind, even as they disavow a desire to dominate it. That the narrower "Christian brotherhood" can reach out to the wider brotherhood of all mankind is thus an even greater creative possibility today than it was in past eras of

Christian history that were dominated by the notion of a "Christendom" into which all men, by whatever means, were supposed to be brought.

The other area, dealing with the relationship of those within the inner Christian brotherhood who have historically become "separated," poses problems of a somewhat different order. Protestants and Catholics share certain things at a very deep level, while still being divided from one another on other deep levels, a fact that is epitomized by the now widely-used phrase, "separated brethren," cited by Fr. Ratzinger in his Postscript. The divisions are not minimized. That the Catholic must look upon his as the "one true church," from which all other Christian bodies are in varying degrees cut off, is directly set forth. That there is a centrality in Catholic theology given to the "office" of hierarchy and priesthood, specifically defined, is another area of basic difference. And that the innermost meaning of Christian brotherhood involves a sense of eucharistic participation which still divides rather than unites us is likewise affirmed. To what degree can "Christian brotherhood" cope with these grievous barriers of separation?

Here is the point at which Fr. Ratzinger's suggestions can be supplemented by the actions of the Second Vatican Council, particularly in the decree *On Ecumenism* and in the constitution *On the Church*. On the first level, that of dogma, while Fr. Ratzinger indicates that "the objective presentation of the vicarious saving act of Jesus Christ can be performed by the one church only," he does point out that there can be grace outside the sacraments and the visible church, though this cannot be allowed to lead to an indeterminate number of churches or sacraments. The further workings of God outside the structure of the Roman Catholic Church are still seen largely in terms of God's making use of individuals in such ways as he may determine.

Vatican II, I believe, has begun to move beyond this and to assert that the grace of God can come to Protestants in their *corporate* life, which possesses some measure (as yet undefined) of ecclesial reality. As the decree puts it, describing all who yearn for unity among Christians, "They do this not merely as individuals but also as members of the corporate groups in which they have heard the Gospel" (Article 1). Even on the liturgical level, God works through, rather than despite, the corporate life of non-Catholic Christians: "The brethren divided from us also carry out many liturgical actions of the Christian religion. In ways that vary according to the condition of each Church or Community, these most certainly can truly engender a life of grace, and, one must say, can aptly give access to the communion of salvation" (Article 3).

The change of descriptive terms (between the second

and third sessions of the Council) from describing Protestants as living in sociological "communities" to describing them as members of "churches and ecclesial communities" opens the door, however equivocally, to a new understanding of the doctrinal relationship of the Roman Catholic Church to Protestant churches. It is the better part of ecumenical sobriety not to pin too much on the phrase (for "churches and ecclesial communities" is deliberately equivocal), but its adoption indicates that the *communal* life of Protestants shares in the *ecclesia* "as a means of salvation"—a status not heretofore clearly acknowledged in Catholic treatment of the separated brethren. If this is not the end of the ecumenical road, it is at least a new beginning.

On the second level, moving from dogma to "concrete human relationships," Fr. Ratzinger points out that since "the immediate brotherly community is made up of the communicants," and that at this precise point our divisions are greatest, our present task is to regard each other as "sisters in the Lord," and to refuse to ignore our present divisions, since to ignore them is to be in danger of becoming complacent about them. Fr. Ratzinger does not put forth a program for the overcoming of division, a fact that is more than understandable in the light of a 1958 dateline. But here, too, the Council decree *On Ecumenism* gives us some guidelines, and mutual attempts to apply them in the future will help us, on both

sides of the divide, to carry on the tasks Fr. Ratzinger
has so clearly defined for us. The theme of mutual peni-
tence for our past sins, for example, has already been
built into the ethos of ecumenically-minded Protestants
and Catholics, in a way that was impossible in 1958,
along with a recognition that inner reform and renewal
are the preconditions of effective ecumenical outreach.

Fr. Ratzinger's essay anticipates two further suggestions of the decree, namely the recognition that both
common dialogue and common action can become
springboards into the ecumenical future. But there is
genuine advance in the decree's other suggestion, that
some beginnings of common worship may characterize
the life of divided Christendom (cf. Article 8). This
may be a more significant *entré* into new explorations of
"Christian brotherhood" than could have been anticipated or even hinted at in 1958, let alone in the early
work of the Second Vatican Council. For while the
conciliar provisions for *communicatio in sacris* do not
extend to the area of sacramental life, and are the most
tentative recommendations of the entire decree, they do
make provision for Catholics and Protestants to begin
to pray together, to sing together, to hear the Word of
God together, and to join in common response to God.
It is already clear that in such experiences they are dis-
covering, even more poignantly than on other levels,
how much they share and how much more tragic, there-

fore, are the things that still keep them from sharing fully.

It may thus turn out, paradoxically but also providentially, that the point of our deepest division will become the point of greatest impetus for the overcoming of division. To endure the cross of separation at this point may be the divinely ordained path toward resurrection in unit.

Robert McAfee Brown

Good Friday, 1966.

Foreword

The following essay was first read to the Theological Congress of the Austrian Institute for Pastoral Work in Vienna at Easter 1958, and subsequently published in *Seelsorger*, 1958, 387–429. This accounts for its historical and factual limitations, as it is intended to be more an invitation to discussion than a definitive treatment of the subject. That such discussion is to be wished for among a wider circle than hitherto is the justification for its publication in a virtually unaltered form.

JOSEPH RATZINGER

Bonn, August 1960.

Abbreviations

Cath	*Catholica*
CCSL	*Corpus Christianorum Series Latina*
CSEL	*Corpus Scriptorum Ecclesiasticorum Latinorum*
DACL	*Dictionnaire d'archéologie chrétienne et de liturgie*
HK	*Herderkorrespondenz*
LTK	*Lexikon für Theologie und Kirche*
MTZ	*Münchener theologische Zeitschrift*
PW-RKA	Pauly and Wissowa, *Realenzyklopadie der klassichen Altertumswissenschaften*
RAC	*Reallexikon für Antike und Christentum*
RGG	*Religion in Geschichte und Gegenwart*
SB-*KNT*	Strack and Billerbeck, *Kommentar zum neuen Testament aus Talmud und Midrash*
TQ	*Theologische Quartalschift*
TWNT	*Theologisches Wörterbuch zum neuen Testament*, ed. V. G. Kittel

AN HISTORICAL ANALYSIS

"You have one teacher, and you are all brethren" (Mt 23:8). These words of Christ define the relationship between Christians as a relationship of brothers, and thus contrast with the natural brotherhood of blood relationship a new brotherhood of the spirit. So the Christian ethos is, or should be, an ethos of brotherliness. In order to grasp the significance, the extent, and the limits of this new brotherhood, we propose examining the various conceptions of brotherhood which are to be found within early Christianity, and those which developed from it later. In this way we shall hope to discover what is specifically Christian about it.

The idea of brotherhood before and outside Christianity

"BROTHER" IN ANCIENT GREECE

Brotherhood is, as we have said, primarily a phenomenon of blood relationship; but the metaphorical use of the term is very old, even if there is not much documentary evidence for it. In Plato we find the description of one's fellow citizen as a brother[1] (*Menexenos*, 239 a): "We and our fellow citizens are all brothers born of one another." Xenophon calls a friend a "brother" (*Anabasis*, II, 2, 25; 38). In the former case, brotherhood is based on the extended blood relationship of a nation; in the latter, on what we may, with Goethe, call an "elective affinity." In both cases brotherhood implies a frontier. In Plato, if the community of the State bestows brotherhood, then the foreigner, the *barbaros*, is re-

[1] Quoted in H. von Soden's article on *adelphos* (brother) in *TWNT*, I, 146, 3 f.; and in K. H. Schelkle's article on *bruder* (brother) in *RAC*, II, 631.

garded as a non-brother; Xenophon's brotherhood of friends not only unites friends, but also divides them off from those who are not friends. All unions involve the separating off of those who are united together from the others. Although neither Plato nor Xenophon specifically refers to it, the basic problem of every brotherhood ethos arises here. If, for example, the people united in one *polis* form a brotherhood, the ethos within that *polis* will necessarily differ from the attitude adopted toward those outside it who are not brothers: ethical responsibility is different within the "extended family" from outside it. In other words, this broadened concept of brotherhood inevitably creates two different kinds of ethos. This is a basic human tension, seen in its most extreme form in the idea of brotherhood, and, as we shall see, in Christianity itself.

THE IDEA OF BROTHERHOOD IN THE OLD TESTAMENT

Whereas we find only scattered references in the Greek world, in Old Testament Israel "brother" was a fixed term of address. Here one's co-religionist generally had the title *ah* (brother).[2] It was the common religion which seemed to be in the forefront of their

[2] Examples in Von Soden, *ibid*, 145; and Schelkle, *ibid*, 635 f.

consciousness here: when merely a compatriot was meant, the word *reʿa* (neighbor) was used[3]; in rabbinical writings the two were sometimes even carefully distinguished. This, it is true, was a later development, for originally the religious community and the national community were one. There is undoubtedly a genuine similarity between the structures of the Greek *polis* and of the theocracy of the Old Testament. In both cases the political unit was taken also as the religious one, and the religious community was the same as the political: the Church was the State, and vice versa.[4] Thus the problem which we have already noted recurs here: the two zones of ethical being, clearly formulated in the two opposed terms *am* and *gojim* ("people" and "Gentiles"). The biblical question, "Who is my neighbor?", is concerned with this very problem.

The particular quality of Old Testament religion colored the problem in a special way. For the individual, a brother was one who belonged with him in the unity not of just any people, but of the unique Chosen People of God. That meant that brotherhood did not depend merely on common racial descent, but on common election by God. It was a brotherhood in which it was

---

[3] Von Soden, *ibid*, 145.

[4] *See* J. Ratzinger, *Volk und Haus Gottes in Augustins Lehre von der Kirche* (Munich, 1954), 255-76.

not the common mother (the *polis?*)[5] which mattered, but the common Father, that is, the universal God, Yahweh. Here we come upon the special charge that the Israelite idea of brotherhood carried. It implied brotherhood with a common Father, God, who was not, however, merely the God of Israel, but the one and only God. And so he was the Father not of Israel alone, but of all.[6] This was the strange paradox of Old Testament religion as a whole: that Israel's national god was the universal God, that, indeed, Israel did not have a national god at all, but a supranational one. This almost implies an impossibility of forming a unity within the brotherhood of one's own nation, or else it could —through a false development—lead to a kind of internal ossification. It all depends on how the connection is seen between this non-national, universal God, on the one hand, and the people who nevertheless worship him as *their* God, on the other. In the Old Testament it is clear that this connection was made not by Israel, but by God, that he chose Israel for no merits of its own,

[5] Concerning the maternal character of the *polis*, *see* Ratzinger, esp. 274. We see it as an idea common to the ancient world in such texts as Gal 4:26: "Jerusalem . . . is our mother."

[6] *See* texts like Ex 4:22; Ps 82, and especially Dt 32:8. For the latter, *see* Quell in *TWNT*, V, 965. For the whole problem, *see* Martin Buber's *An der Wende: Reden uber das Judentum*, Cologne-Olten 1952; J. Daniélou, *The Lord of History* (London, 1958), 59–71, with further examples.

but by a free decision of his grace, and that he could therefore freely reject it (for which all its subsequent transgressions would provide more than sufficient justification).[7] Thus God had a special paternity toward Israel: whereas he was the Father of all the peoples of the world through the Creation, he was beyond that the Father of Israel through election.[8] But this special situation was the free disposition of God, and it could therefore be altered at any time. This brought an element of uncertainty into any tendency to separate off the brotherly community of Israel too rigidly. In fact, the Prophets always tried to arouse this sense of the potential openness of the Israelite religion both in their prophecies of doom to Israel and in their prophecies of salvation. These always opened on to a universal horizon.

The other possibility implicit in the basic paradox of the Jewish idea of God was made explicit in later Judaism. As the process of rationalizing the whole conception of religion developed, a free and uncaused elective decision by God no longer seemed appropriate. Thus the idea was born that, though God had offered all the peoples of the world the Torah, only Israel had

[7] This idea of possible rejection is a basic theme of all the prophets down to John the Baptist (Mt 3:9). The idea of free election is particularly well expressed in Ezek 6:1–14.

[8] *See* the references given in footnote 1.

accepted it and had thus become the unique People of God.[9] In the last analysis, this means that it was not God who chose Israel, but Israel who was the only people to take God as its god. By this time, however, the idea that the God of the people was in fact the God of the universe no longer had the effect of "opening up" Israel; on the contrary, it led to an even stricter sealing-off from those who voluntarily renounced the special paternity of God and, therefore, the brotherly love of his children. We are here at the threshold which separates the Old Testament as *praeparatio evangelica* from Judaism as the "synagogue." In both cases, however, we can see the new tension (new, that is, as compared with Greek ideas) created by the ethos of brotherhood through subordination to the paternity of the universal God.

This tension comes into the Old Testament concept of brotherhood because of its idea of God, and it has a parallel within its idea of man. Over against the "closed" community which comes from Abraham, Isaac, and Jacob, there stands the universal horizon of biblical history which, at root, is not simply a history of Israel, but sets the history of Israel within the universal history

[9] *See* SB-*KNT*, III, Munich 1954², 139 ff.; G. F. Moore, *Judaism*, I (Cambridge, 1927), 274 ff. The corresponding Haggadic idea is found in (among other sources) Philo, Baruch's Apocalypse, 4 Ezra, and the Talmud.

of the one humanity. All men, Israelites and Gentiles, ultimately constituted a single humanity because of their single human source and the single creative act of God.

This unity of all men is shown twice: once in the Creation, in which God formed "Adam" (that is, mankind), the root of all the other men to come, in his likeness; and a second time in Noah, with whom a new race of men is started after the catastrophe of the first race. The genealogies of Genesis 10 endeavor to prove in detail that the whole of historical humanity owes its existence to God's saving covenant of grace with Noah and can live only under the constant care of God assured in that covenant.[10] On the other hand, it still remains that God made a special covenant with Abraham which separates the children of Abraham as a special family from the great human family of the children of Adam (or, rather, of Noah). Thus we can see that both the unity and the duality of the ethos have as their two starting points the image of God and the image of man. The *unity* it attested by the uniqueness of God and the common father of mankind, Adam or Noah (both of whom create a religious community of men insofar as both are accorded a lasting relationship with God: the likeness to God in the case of Adam; the covenant with God in the case of Noah); the *duality* comes from the

[10] *See* the commentaries on Genesis; e.g., B. H. Junker, *Genesis*, (Wurzburg, 1949), 36; G. von Rad, *Genesis* (London, 1961), 135ff.

elective exclusiveness of God toward Israel and the exclusive descent from the fathers of the covenant, Abraham, Isaac, and Jacob.

In practical terms, this meant that direct brotherhood applied only to those who shared one's country and faith. The ethical responsibility an Israelite bore toward another Israelite was different from that he bore toward a Gentile. Thus there were two kinds of ethical relationship here: my neighbor is distinct from a man who is far from me; my brother is distinct from my fellow man. To the question, "Who is my neighbor?", there was a simple and clear answer: "My co-religionist and compatriot." This evident and undeniable duality could never degenerate into dualism, however, as was possible in the Greek world and in the religions of the countries surrounding Israel; rather, it was held together through the unity of God and through the unity of humanity, so that human responsibility went beyond the framework of the brotherly community, as is shown concretely by the Old Testament's laws concerning strangers (Ex 22:20; 23:9; Dt 14:29, and elsewhere; Lv 19:33 f.; 19:10; 23:22; Num 9:14; 15:14 ff.; 35:15).[11] But in order to understand correctly the relationship between these two zones of ethics, it is important to note the dualities of brothers in the Old Testament. At important

[11] *See* also the article "Fremde" (stranger) in H. Haag, *Bibel-Lexikon* (Einsiedeln, 1951), 495, and the appropriate section of the article *xenos* (stranger) by G. Stahlin in *TWNT*, V, 8–16.

points of salvation history there appear pairs of brothers, the election or rejection of each of whom is strangely connected. These are, in particular, Cain and Abel (and Cain and Seth), Ishmael and Isaac, Esau and Jacob. That this is a theologically planned pattern seems clear, particularly as in one place we read that Abraham had a number of other sons apart from Isaac and Ishmael (Gen 25:1–6).[12] The full meaning of this "theology of the two brothers," as one may call it, becomes clear only in the New Testament and the Fathers. Nevertheless we can still see here that even the partners of Israel who were expelled from the election could yet be understood in a wider sense as "brothers," that even he who was rejected remained a "brother"—especially when rejection and election are switched in such a strange way as with Esau and Jacob, that is, with the definitive establishment of the line of election. This raises a question which was never answered in the Old Testament itself but was to become all the more important for the New Testament.

THE DEVELOPMENT IN HELLENISM

After these brief remarks on the idea of brotherhood in the Old Testament, let us go back to the Greek world. The breakup of the *polis* and its religion after

---

[12] *See* Karl Barth's view of election, outlined briefly in the second part, for an understanding of this pattern.

the Macedonian period had necessarily led to the formation of new communities, and these were, in fact, religious in nature. The influence of the East was of great significance. In the Syrian Baal cults, the tribes and groups who were united through blood and the unity of the protective deity had long regarded themselves as sons of this god and as brothers of one another.[13] A foreigner also could become part of this brotherhood after undergoing an initiation ceremony. We find the same thing in the closely allied Syrian Jupiter cults, in the cult of the Magna Mater, and in the Jewish syncretistic communities of the Crimea which considered themselves as brothers because of the common "highest God." The term "brother" was most used in the Mithras community whose hierarchic head bore the name *pater* or *pater patrum*, whereas the other celebrants of the rite were called *fratres*. Similar developments took place in late Judaism as well when splinter groups broke off from the main community. Thus we know from Josephus that the Essenes called themselves brothers, and the members of the Qumran sect(who were perhaps identical with the Essenes) did so as well.

The Qumran sect also used the term "sister" by analogy. Within the Christian Church also we find the breaking away of more strictly organized fraternal com-

[13] Documentation for the following in Schelkle, 633–6. *See* also Von Soden, 146,1 ff.

munities, such as the Moravian brethren.[14] A double ethos was again developed through such brotherhoods as they owed their very existence to the desire to form a narrower human and religious community, when the political community and the traditional main church had become too big and unmanageable. But what might at first have seemed merely the result of personal free choice became, in the mystery cults, raised to the mystical and ontological level by the idea of rebirth. In this way the new brotherhood acquired increased importance, and the dividing-off from others was, in a particular way, strictly carried through; the protective wall of the secret discipline separated the initiated from the uninitiated clearly and emphatically.

An extreme example of the development of the double ethos was the Roman law-case concerning Bacchanalia in 186 B.C., in which a mystery group was prosecuted by the state as a criminal organization: the inner ethos of this community involved a criminal attitude toward the rest of the world.[15] As we know, the

[14] *See* RGG, I[3], 1435 ff. The process begins, in a sense, naturally within the Church itself with the formation of monastic communities and "brotherhoods." Concerning the general phenomenon in religious history of the special brotherhood, *see* the article on *Geheimbunde* (secret societies) by A. Closs, *Religions-weissenschaftliches Wörterbuch*, ed. F. König (Freiburg, 1956), 279 ff.

[15] *See* A. Kolping, *Sacramentum Tertullianeum* (Munster, 1948), 32 ff.; PW-*RKA*, XVI, 2 (1935), 1305 f.

early Christians were persecuted by the Roman State for the same reason: a secret society whose mystic ethos seemed criminal to those outside.

Simultaneous with this development of new, narrowly circumscribed fraternities, there was also an exactly opposite development. Political unification had its philosophical parallel in Stoic cosmopolitanism which discovered the unity of the world and of men. Epictetus saw all men as brothers, for all came from God.[16] The ideas of the Stoa, of Seneca, Musonius, and Marcus Aurelius, followed the same direction.[17] Thus one basic ethos of brotherliness was appropriate to all men. In the Hermes mystery cult this idea of the universal paternity of God and of the brotherhood of his children—mankind—found a direct religious expression. The uninitiated were the "ignorant brothers," whom the enlightened remembered when they prayed to the Father. "Fill me with thy strength," the mystic prayed, "and then I shall enlighten with this grace those of my people who live in ignorance, my brothers, your children."[18]

[16] E. Zeller, *Outlines of the History of Greek Philosophy* (London, 1931), 269 ff.

[17] Zeller, 266 ff.; 268 *n.* 1; 269; 271.

[18] *Corpus Hermeticum*, 1, 32, quoted in Schelkle, 634. The whole text is translated in O. Casel, *Das Gedachtnis des Herrn*, 1919, 44 ff.

THE ENLIGHTENMENT AND MARXISM

The idea of a single, all-embracing brotherhood resounded strongly in the period of eighteenth-century Enlightenment, and it is in the thought of this time that it found its most radical and effective form. The French Revolution proclaimed *liberté, egalité, fraternité,* and made the brotherhood of men with equal rights a political, revolutionary program. The origin of this brotherhood in the common paternity of God now moved very much into the background. It has too remote, too hypothetical a ring when Schiller sings in his *Ode to Joy,* "Brothers, above the starry sky there must dwell a loving father"; the brotherhood of man seems independent of this idea. It is conceived as coming from this world, from the similar heredity and nature of all men. It involves going behind history to the nature of man that is anterior to it.[19] All differences between men come from positive action, that is, from man's wilful behavior in history. They are what Kant calls something merely "statutory," whereas before and above them stands the natural equality of all. The re-establishment and the continuing respect for natural equality

[19] *See* G. Söhngen, "Vom Wesen des Christentums," *Die Einheit in der Theologie* (Munich, 1952), 288–304. He interprets the Enlightenment as a radical liberation of man from history.

—the original brotherhood of *all* men—was the aim of the French Revolution. We must assist original nature to be victorious over the subsequent misdealings of history. The question whether history can really be subordinated to nature in this way was never asked.

As can be seen, the problem of the extended idea of brotherhood was here solved in a very radical way: brotherhood no longer created two separate zones of ethical behavior; on the contrary, in the name of brotherhood all barriers were removed and a unified ethos was proclaimed as binding on all men in equal measure. This sweeping away of all divisions has something splendid about it, but it is dearly bought, for brotherhood, extended so far, becomes unrealistic and meaningless. The naïveté of Schiller's "Be embraced ye millions" has often been remarked on in this connection. In fact, a brotherliness which embraces everyone equally cannot expect to be taken seriously by anyone. This insight rather deepens the problem we have set ourselves, for it raises these questions: Must an ethos, to be realizable, perhaps contain some form of duality? Does it inevitably require a closed "inner ring" to be fully workable? We should remember here that the program of the Enlightenment did not emerge very well as realized through the French Revolution which differentiated drastically and bloodily between the inner fraternal circle of the revolutionaries and the outer circle of the non-revolutionaries; and we must remember that liberalism, the heir of the Enlightenment ideology, also created in freemasonry its own highly differentiated inner fraternal group.

From the Enlightenment the path leads directly to the Marxist idea of fraternity. That the word "comrade" is preferred to "brother" is of secondary importance, although it does indicate a different emphasis in Marxist ideology. The idea of God as the common father has finally disappeared, but the idea of common humanity has also lost some of its importance through the commitment to a socialist community. What most distinguishes Marxism from the thinking of the Enlightenment is the decisive return to the idea of two ethical zones, here carried through with a radicality unparalleled in history. No longer is there any idea of the equal brotherhood of all men; rather, humanity is divided into two totally antithetical groups, capital and proletariat, and their embattled dialectic constitutes what history is. Fate and, to some extent, his own decision puts a man—as we have already suggested—on one or the other side of divided humanity. Whichever side he is on, however, man has to accept this division as given. It provides him with the law of his human behavior. He cannot treat all men as brothers, but only some; the others are enemies. If he loves one group, he is forced to side with them and fight the others. Hence Marxism involves, from the beginning, a division of the world, intended by Marx as a purely social division; now—as a result of the Russian Revolution and of world politics—Marxism has become a political division into two opposing blocks of states. However little this may correspond to Marx's original conception, it is a logical development from it. Brotherhood toward some involves enmity toward others.

This dualism, of course, is not the last word about Marxism. Rather does the present struggle of divided mankind take place in the hope of its eschatological reunion in the condition of the classless society. But this reunion lies beyond history; it is the enduring final condition of mankind. Here we come upon an idea that is shared with the Enlightenment: for Marxism, too, the division of mankind is given historically, the fall away of history from nature, the self-alienation of man. But Marxism has a far clearer idea of the nature of this self-alienation than the Enlightenment, and above all it seeks the conquest of this historical alienation— the return to pure nature—not in a vague, emotional idea of universal brotherhood, but in the stern discipline of a hard and purposeful fight. The goal is also the unified, undifferentiated brotherhood of all men; but the way is the limited brotherhood of the Socialist Party, the acknowledgement of a divided humanity.[20]

So far we have outlined the most important non-Christian forms of the idea of brotherhood. It is obvious that each of the conceptions we have described has some relationship to Christianity. Some of them were even confused with Christian ideas, or regarded themselves as true Christianity; conceptions as different from each other as the Enlightenment's ethos of universal brotherhood and the closed world of the mysteries were equated with Christianity. The confusion between the brotherly love of the Enlightenment and the universal Christian love of one's neighbor, at least in some of its forms, is still more widely disseminated than one might think. On the other hand, the researches of Otto Casel in our century have given renewed cause to see Christianity, in terms of the phenomenology of religion, under the *eidos* of the mystery cult—that is, as a religious type of the mystery cov-

---

[20] Apart from the basic work by G. A. Wetter, *Dialectical Materialism: A Historical and Systematic Survey of Philosophy in the Soviet Union* (London, 1958), *see* the instructive essay by J. Lacroix, "Der marxistische Mensch," *Dokumente* 1948, vols. 1 and 2, and K. Löwith, *Weltgeschichte und Heilsgeschehen* (Stuttgart, 1953), 38–54.

enant.[21] Whether one or the other or neither is correct is obviously of central importance for determining the idea of Christian brotherhood. Vice versa, we can also see that an understanding of the Christian idea of brotherhood is not just peripheral, but can contribute greatly to a correct typological formulation of the Christian religion.

[21] A comprehensive survey of Casel's work can be found in T. Filthaut, *Die Kontroverse uber die Mysterienlehre* (Warendorf, 1947). See particularly 86–98 for our question below.

The development of the idea of brotherhood in early Christianity

"BROTHER" IN THE WORDS OF CHRIST

Before we can attempt a comprehensive factual and dogmatic definition of the Christian idea of brotherhood, it seems necessary to set out simply what is given historically in the New Testament and the Fathers.

When we examine the appropriate texts in the New Testament, the first thing we notice is that, at least in terminology, there is no one consistent idea of brotherhood that goes through them all. In the early texts the Jewish terminology is simply taken over[1]; but at the same time there starts to develop, first tentatively but ever more independently, a Christian use of the term which finally, by the latest texts of Scripture —that is, in John—is totally distinct (1 Jn 2:9, 10;

[1] Schelkle, op. cit., 636, quotes as examples of this Jewish usage Ac 2:29, 37; 7:2; 13:15, 26; 22:1, 5; 28:15, 21; Jas 1:9; 2:15; 4:11; Mt 5:22, 24, 47; 7:3, 4, 5; 18:15, 21, 35.

3:10, 16, 17; 5:16; 3 Jn 3, 5, 10).[2] Here we come upon the problem, explored particularly by Dutch philologists, of the special language of the early Christians.[3] Here, too, we can see how the idea of "brother" which was further developed in the Fathers, but then became quickly less important. This linguistic process is of great interest, because in it we can see, in a particularly tangible way, how the Christian community gradually developed to become an independent church, how early Christianity grew and became firmly grounded. Let us start with Christ's use of the word "brother." Schelkle distinguishes in his utterances three chief usages. The first group of texts simply takes over the Old Testament Jewish use: by "brother" is meant one's *Jewish* co-religionist. All these texts are to be found in Matthew's Gospel.

[2] As we shall see, one should probably also include some of the Matthew texts here as well, which may well reflect the perfected terminology of a Christian community rather than the formulations of Christ before the separation from the Jewish fraternal community.

[3] *See*, in particular, the work of C. Mohrmann, especially *Die altchristliche Sondersprache in den Sermones des hl. Augustin*, I (Nijmegen, 1932). Also important is H. Janssen's *Kultur und Sprache: zur Geschichte der alten Kirche im Spiegel de Sprachentwicklung—Von Tertullian bis Cyprian* (Nijmegen, 1938). A critical discussion of the question of a special language can be found in H. Becker, *Tertullians Apologeticum: Werden und Leistung* (Munich, 1954), 335–45.

You have heard that it was said to the men of old. "You shall not kill; and whoever kills shall be liable to judgment." But I say to you that every one who is angry with his brother shall be liable to judgment." But I say to you that brother shall be liable to the council, and whoever says, "You fool!" shall be liable to the hell of fire. So if you are offering your gift at the altar, and there remember that your brother has something against you, leave your gift there before the altar and go; first be reconciled to your brother; and then come and offer your gift [5:21–4].

Why do you see the speck that is in your brother's eye, but do not notice the log that is in your own eye? (7:3; *cf.* 7:4–5)

If your brother sins against you, go and tell him his fault, between you and him alone. If he listens to you, you have gained your brother. But if he does not listen, take one or two others along with you, that every word may be confirmed by the evidence of two or three witnesses. If he refuses to listen to them, tell it to the church; and if he refuses to listen even to the church, let him be to you as a Gentile and a tax collector (18:15 ff.; cf. 18:21 about how often to forgive, and 18:35: "So also my heavenly Father will do to every one of you, if you do not forgive your brother from your heart.").

In the important text of Mt 18:15 ff., at any rate, we must assume a strong influence from the usage of the community,[4] and this is probably the case with the other texts as well.[5] This means that these texts do not give us directly the terminology of Christ, but of the Jewish Christian community, thus representing an already comparatively settled condition of Christian usage. However, the word "brother" in this connection could certainly go back to Jesus himself, as is suggested by the comparison between Mt 18:15 ff. and Lk 17:3. In this case the developed community of St Matthew's Gospel, because of their new situation, would have understood something else in the words of Jesus than was originally directly intended—the new Christian brotherly community, rather than the old Jewish religious and national community. This reinterpretation was possible because of the analogy between both groups; following Jesus, a new religious community had developed which resembled in structure the old Jewish religious community. Nevertheless, in this first group of texts from the mouth of Jesus we

[4] *See* J. Schmid, *Das Evangelium nach Matthaus* (Regensburg New Testament, 1), 1956[3], 271 ff.

[5] Certainly this seems clear in 5:23 ff. This text is understood in the *Didache*, XIV, 2, as a rule of the community, and was probably also understood as such when it was taken into Greek Matthew.

meet, not his own new message of brotherhood, but either the language of a Christian community that is already fairly developed or else words of Jesus which merely take over the language of his Jewish environment.

A second group of texts comprises those of his utterances in which he does not follow the general Jewish usage, but the special use of the word "brother" which the rabbis used to describe their pupils. To this group Schelkle ascribes the well-known words of Christ to Peter at the Last Supper: "Simon, Simon, behold, Satan demanded to have you, that he might sift you like wheat, but I have prayed for you that your faith may not fail; and when you have turned again, strengthen your brethren" (Lk 22:31). Two utterances of the risen Christ also belong in this group. One is the words, recorded by Matthew, that he addressed to the women who were the first to meet him, when he told them to "go and tell my brethren to go to Galilee, and there they will see me" (Mt 28:10). The other, found in John, opens up deeper theological perspectives, and thus transcends the rabbinical framework. Here he tells Mary Magdalene, "go to my brethren and say to them, I am ascending to my Father and your Father, to my God and your God" (Jn 20:17b). The brotherhood of the disciples among one another and with Christ is here closely connected with the father-

49

hood of God, and thus raised to a quite different level than the mere teacher-pupil relationship which the rabbinical use of "brother" signified. Schelkle is right to include here too, at least formally, the important words of Jesus in Mt 22:8, which could well be the motto of our investigation: "You are not to be called rabbi, for you have one teacher, and you are all brethren."[6] It is, however, clear that in content this sentence implies the end of rabbinism, the Christian revolution, the lessening of all worldly distinctions in the face of the encounter with the one who is truly great, truly different—Christ. Thus in these words which formally represent rabbinical usage, there breaks through the new Christian idea of brotherhood. Indeed, perhaps all the texts of this second group represent a progression toward the definitive Christian usage. Formally it is rabbinical if the master (i.e., rabbi) calls his disciples his brothers; but in order to assess the implications of this for the future, it is necessary to consider the self-awareness of this particular master and the consciousness that he had of the importance of his disciples. On the latter point in particular the gospels leave us in no doubt; when Jesus chose twelve disciples, he chose a symbolic number whose significance was obvious for every reader of Scripture. He places himself in the posi-

[6] Schelkle, *op. cit.*, 636. We find also the rabbinical usage in 1 Tim 5:1.

tion of Jacob and his twelve sons who became the
twelve patriarchs of the Chosen People of Israel; in this
way he showed that here a new, truer "Israel" was beginning. The twelve, who were not called apostles to
start with, but only *hoi dodeka*, are marked out by
their number as the spiritual patriarchs of a new, spiritual People of God.[7]

When Jesus calls his disciples "brothers," then, it is
something quite different from when an ordinary rabbi
speaks of his pupils. It is making a decision for the
future, for in these twelve the new People of God is
being addressed; in them it is being designated as a
people of brothers, a great new brotherhood. In other
words, in the eyes of Jesus the twelve are not a group
of rabbinical pupils (just as he did not regard himself
as a rabbi), but correspond to the people of Israel,
symbolize it at a higher level, and recapitulate the
brotherhood of the old Israel which we were consider-
ing before.

Let us now proceed to the third group of texts in
which Jesus uses the word "brother." This time it is
a typically Christian usage. Schelkle mentions here

---

[7] *See* F. M. Braun, *Neues Licht auf die Kirche* (Einsiedeln
1946), 71; A. Fridrichsen, "Messias und Kirche," *Ein buch von der
Kirche*, ed. Aulén, Fridrichsen, Nygren, and others (Göttingen
1951), 33. *See* especially K. H. Rengstorf's article on *dodeka* in
TWNT, II, 321–8.

particularly Mk 3:31–5. When told that his mother and his brothers are outside, Jesus replied, " 'Who are my mother and my brothers?' And looking around on those who sat about him, he said, 'Here are my mother and my brothers! Whoever does the will of God is my brother, and sister, and mother.' " In the place of blood relationship, and surpassing it, is set spiritual relationship. For Jesus, brothers are those who are united with him in the common acceptance of the will of God[8] The difference from the ideology of the Enlightenment and the general brotherhood of the Stoics is obvious: brotherhood is not seen naturalistically, as an original phenomenon of nature, but depends on a decision of the spirit, a saying "yes" to the will of God.

The second text to which Schelkle refers here is more influenced by the terminology of the community. It is Mk 10:29 where Jesus promises to him who leaves his brothers, sisters, father, mother, children, or lands for his sake and in order to preach the gospel, the return of all he had left even in this life, even though there would be persecutions as well. It is surely true to say that the new and greater family that is here prom-

[8] Similarly Jn 14:21: "He who has my commandments and keeps them, he it is who loves me; and he who loves me will be loved by my Father." Also 15:14 ff. It is notable that John here replaces the word *adelphos* (brother) by *philos* (friend), and that the fourth gospel uses the word *adelphos* outside the meaning of blood relationship only in two places: 20:17 and 21:23.

ised to the missionary is composed of the members of the Christian communities looked after by him. This is, in fact, the same idea as before, only more strongly influenced by the idea of an already existent Christian community. It follows that the community of will with the Father is conceived more concretely, too, as acceptance of the Christian faith.

In the great judgment parable of Mt 25:31–46 we find a quite different conception of the Christian idea of brotherhood. The difference is so marked that it can hardly be grouped with any of the texts we have considered hitherto.[9] The judge of the world declares to those gathered before his tribunal that the works of mercy done (or not done) for those in need were done (or not done) for himself, and he calls these people in need "the least of these my brethren" (25:40). Nothing suggests that only the faithful, only believers in the gospel of Christ, are meant here, as is the case in a similar text (Mk 9:41), but rather all people in need, without differentiation.[10] On the other hand, it is not permissible to conclude from the expression "the least of these my brethren" that the judge of the world is calling all men his brothers, and among them those in

[9] Schelkle, *op. cit.*, 637, places it in the third group, which is justified inasmuch as it is a specifically Christian text. Within this group, however, it has a unique position.
[10] Thus Schmid, 355.

need. A large number of texts show that Christ sees himself generally represented in the poor and lowly especially, people who—quite apart from their ethical quality, but simply through their being lowly, and the appeal to the love of others that lies in that—make present the master.[11] Instead of calling them "the least of [his] brethren," it would be more correct to translate: "my brothers (i.e., the least)." The *elakhistoi* are, as such, the brothers of the Lord who has made himself the least of men.[12] Brotherhood with Christ is founded here not, as before, on the freely chosen community of will and conviction, but on the community of lowliness and suffering. This text is important because it expresses a universality which does not exist in what we have considered hitherto. If the community of the disciples is the basis of a new Israel, and thus of a new fraternal community, then we might expect that the closed brotherhood of Israel would repeat itself once more. The question, "Who is my neighbor?", would then receive a different answer, but structurally

[11] This appears clearly from the frequent emphasis of the *mikroi* (lowly, humble). See Mt 10:42; 11:11; 18:6, 10. See also O. Michel's article on *mikros* in the *TWNT*, IV, 650–6.

[12] Compare the idea of Jesus as the Son of Man, in which both Daniel's idea of sovereignty and Isaiah's idea of the remnant are combined. *See* J. Schmid, *Das Evangelium nach Markus* (Regensburg New Testament, 2), 1954[3], 160 ff. *See* also the important Marcan text 10:41–5, and the washing of the feet, Jn 13:1–20.

it would be the same as the old one. One's neighbor would now no longer be one's compatriot, one's co-religionist in an essentially national faith, but the fellow believer in the non-political, spiritual faith of Christ. He who has read the judgment parable of Mt 25 knows why the answer of Jesus is different in the parable of the Good Samaritan (Lk 10:30–7). My neighbor is the first man I meet who is in need, for, as such, he is simply a brother of the master who is always present to me in the lowliest of men. This raises the question whether, in these texts (Mt 25:31–46 and Lk 10:30–7) which we spontaneously feel to be the most sublime, the unlimited brotherhood of the Enlightenment—at least in its purest forms, such as in Lessing's *Nathan*—is not in fact fulfilled? It is true that there is here an ultimate removal of barriers which one finds in so complete a form only in Stoicism and the Enlightenment. Nevertheless, there is in the gospel a Christological element in the idea of brotherhood which creates a quite different spiritual atmosphere from the Enlightenment ideology. But even apart from this, the other texts remain which, unlike this last and open idea of brotherhood, suggest a more or less closed one. Thus the brotherhood texts which proceed from the mouth of Jesus present us with an open question. On the one hand, it is clear that all those who need help are, irrespective of any barriers, through their very plight the brothers of Jesus. On the other hand, it is also apparent that the coming community of the faithful will form a new fraternal community which will be distinct from those who do not believe. Thus we have a limited conception on one side, and a universal one on the other. It remains unresolved how they are related to each other.

THE DEVELOPMENT WITHIN THE NEW TESTAMENT, ESPECIALLY IN PAUL

If we turn now to the development of the idea of brotherhood in the community Jesus left behind, we come first upon a simple adoption of the national, religious formula of the Jews. Both Peter and Stephen call the Jews in their sermons *andres adelphoi* (brethren: [Ac 2:29; 7:2]); Paul is so addressed by the Jews (13:15), and himself addresses them as such (13:26; 22:1, 22:5; 28:17; compare the interesting text Rom 9:3, in which the changing of the meaning is clear). However, Acts also refers quite naturally to the Christians as brothers wherever it is the editor himself writing (14:2; 28:15).[13] Schelkle considers Jewish those

[13] Schelkle, *op. cit.*, 636, considers that this text is an example of the Jewish usage; but that it is more appropriately to be regarded as the terminology of the Christian community is shown by A. Wikenhauser in his *Die Apostelgeschichte* (Regensburg New Testament, 5), 1956[3], 285.

texts of James that use the word *adelphos* (1:9; 2:15; 4:11). Here I think one must say that by "brother" is meant one's fellow Christian, but that in fact the community of James had simply taken over this usage from the Jewish mother church, and that this community had apparently not yet achieved complete separation from Judaism. To this extent we can say that the use of the idea of brother does not here have a markedly Christian stamp.

Its decisive Christian emphasis is the work of Paul for whom it followed naturally from the development of Christianity as something independent of Judaism, which was his life's work. Indeed, the new emphasis in the idea of brother is ultimately a necessary linguistic side-effect of this struggle for a concrete historical separating-out of the Christian. "Brother," for Paul, is the natural name of one's *Christian* fellow believer, and we find it in a great many texts.[14] The word *pseudadelphos* ("false brother") is actually a word coined by Paul in which he expresses the sad experience of his missionary work and sets the limits of Christian brotherhood.[15] We shall not find a developed theory of

[14] These texts can easily be found with help of a concordance. Schelkle's observation is interesting: the word "brother," though found frequently in the chief epistles, occurs only rarely in the pastoral epistles.

[15] Schelkle, *op. cit.*, 638; see 2 Cor 11:26; Gal 2:4.

Christian brotherhood in Paul, but he does offer a number of important new ideas for it. The most important one is found in Rom 8:14–17, 29:

> For all who are led by the Spirit of God are sons of God. For you did not receive the spirit of slavery to fall back into fear, but you have received the spirit of sonship. When we cry, "Abba! Father!" it is the Spirit himself bearing witness with our spirit that we are children of God, and if children, then heirs, heirs of God and fellow heirs with Christ . . . For those whom he foreknew he also predestined to be conformed to the image of his Son, in order that he might be the first-born among many brethren.

Heb 2:11 is related to this text: "For he who sanctifies and those who are sanctified have all one origin. That is why he is not ashamed to call them brethren." This provides the theological anchor of the Christian conception of brotherhood. If the brotherhood of Israel depended on the special paternity of God which was given in its election, then in Christianity the idea of fatherhood is made more profound through the Trinity. The fatherhood of God refers in the first place to *the* Son, Christ, and then through him to us, since his spirit is in us and says "Father" in us (Rom 8:16).[16] The fatherhood of God, then, is a fatherhood mediated to us through Christ in the Spirit. God is primarily the Father of Christ; but we are "in Christ," and are so through the Holy Spirit.[17] We can see here how the Jewish idea of the Father is transformed and intensified in Christianity. Fatherhood, and with it brotherhood, gains a far greater depth of meaning; it points beyond the act of *will* involved in election toward a union which affects our very being.

After we had established that the idea of God the Father was necessary for the conception of brotherhood, we saw that the Adam-Noah-Abraham teaching in Jewish thought was its other anchor. This doctrine, too, is reinterpreted by Paul in a Christian sense, which also had an influence on the idea of brotherhood. In place of the simple Adam story of Genesis—which, moreover, even in its gnostic commutations, had remained a one-Adam story—Paul develops in 1 Cor 15 and Rom 5 his doctrine of the two Adams. Christ,

---

[16] The close connection between Christ and the Spirit, which is essential for this argument, is stated by Paul in the succinct formula "The Lord is the Spirit" (2 Cor 3:17). *See* P. van Imschoot's article on "Geist Gottes" ("the Spirit of God") in H. Haag's *Bibellexikon*, 531–40 (especially 537).

[17] *See* A. Oepke's article on *en* (in) in the *TWNT*, II, 534–9.

having passed through the death of the first Adam, becomes in the resurrection a new, second Adam, the Father of a new and better humanity. Thus with Christ there begins not only a new humanity, but also a new human brotherhood, which surpasses and replaces the old. For the old brotherhood of Adam is, in the eyes of Paul—who looks back at it from the new Adam, Christ —merely a fraternity of evil and, therefore, not worth seeking after. Only the new brotherhood, which is also universal in its tendency, brings a true unity of salvation. We can see how the doctrine of the two Adams implies a marked criticism of the humanity ideal of the Enlightenment, by accepting only the second humanity, that of the "last man," Christ (1 Cor 15:45). Its brotherhood *is not yet* universal, but it seeks to become so.[18] Men, in general, *are not yet* brothers in Christ, but they can and must become so. While the doctrine of the two Adams, despite its universal tendency, must involve in the concrete a certain limitation of brotherhood (which, however, may never be seen as a closed, but always as an open brotherhood), in the new version of the Abraham doctrine the impression of delimitation predominates. This doc-

[18] The word "brother" is not used in this connection, but it is an obvious implication through the whole of Paul's thinking at this point.

trine had hitherto declared the closed and special nature of Israel, but Paul bursts asunder even this special nature and proclaims as the true children of Abraham. independently of any national privilege, all those who have the faith of Abraham, that is, who are in Christ Jesus (Rom 4; Gal 3:16–29; 4:21–31). Nevertheless, even here the delimitation is not boundless. In place of the national barrier we now have the spiritual barrier between faith and unbelief. It is important to note that neither Paul nor any other New Testament author founded Christian brotherhood on rebirth, in the sense of the mystery religions; it is certainly a viewpoint possible in a comprehensive account of the implications of New Testament thinking, and we do find it in the Fathers; however, the New Testament itself does not itself formulate these implications. Perhaps this may be mere chance; nevertheless, it is a fact which is not unimportant for our understanding of the character of New Testament religion. It shows that neither Paul, nor anyone else in the New Testament, understood the Christian community according to the analogy of a mystery brotherhood. This community is far more public than a mystery group. It sees itself not in analogy with the more or less private mystery groups, but in analogy with the people of Israel—indeed, with humanity. It claims to be the true Israel, and the germ cell of the new mankind.[19] Its new brotherhood is to be understood from this claim.

From what we have said so far, it is clear that the old problem inherent in the idea of brotherhood is posed again with Paul: the problem of the two zones of ethical attitudes. Despite all delimitation and universalism, the idea of brotherhood is, as we have seen, by no means simply generalized. Every man *can* become a Christian, but only he who really does is a brother. The effect of this situation is shown in the ethical terminology of the apostle. The attitude of *agapé* (love) is appropriate toward every man, but *philadelphia* (brotherly love) only toward one's fellow Christian.[20] The use of this idea for those other than blood relations seems to be specifically Christian.[21] But it shows very clearly that the Christians together form an inner ring in their ethos, that they are (or should be) held together by a spirit of brotherly love which is even greater than that of the general *agape*. This idea is clearly expressed in a number of texts,

[19] This public claim of the church has been worked out particularly by E. Peterson. *See* his essays "Die Kirche" and "Der Monotheismus als politisches Problem," in *Theologische Traktate* (Munich, 1951), 409–28 and 45–147 respectively.

[20] H. Schurmann, "Gemeinde als Bruderschaft im Lichte des Neuen Testaments," *Diaspora, Gabe und Aufgabe* (Paderborn, 1955), 21–31 (esp. 27).

[21] Von Soden, *op. cit.*, 146, 20 f.

particularly in Gal 6:10: "let us do good to all men, and especially to those who are of the household of faith."[22] Closely related to this passage is a text from 1 Pt 2:17: "Honor all men. Love the brotherhood."[23] The brotherhood of Christians, which arises in the first instance from the removal of the barriers of the Jewish fraternal community, fixes its own frontiers with increasing distinctness as the young church gradually takes charge. Within the brotherhood itself this results in a widespread tearing down of all dividing barriers. The existing social order is not changed, it is true, but the Epistle to Philemon (and also 1 Tim) shows us how unimportant they have become: the Christian master must see his brother in the Christian slave (Phil 16), and Christian slaves are exhorted not to despise their Christian masters, because their masters are also their brothers (1 Tim 6:2). If we compare these texts with similar passages in Epictetus, the superiority of the limited brotherhood over the general ideal of humanity is clear: it creates a true relationship, whereas the other remains an empty ideal.

---

[22] *See* also 1 Cor 6:5, 8 and Schurmann. Many examples are quoted in Sladeczek's article, "*He philadelphia* [brotherly love] nach den Schriften des hl. Apostels Paulus," *TQ*, 76 (1894), 272–95.

[23] For the special Christian meaning of *adelphotes* (the concrete fraternal community) see von Soden, 146, 14 f., and Schelkle, 638.

In the Johannine writings the Christian idea of brotherhood finds its final form. Not only is the word "brother" here restricted to one's fellow Christian; it is particularly striking that John always demands brotherly love, the love of Christians for one another, but never speaks of the love of all men.[24] The communities, which are now distinguishable from all other previous human groupings as something new and different, tend obviously to a certain exclusivity. This is clearly shown by a text such as 3 Jn 5–8: "Beloved, it is a loyal thing you do when you render any service to the brethren, especially to strangers, who have testified to your love before the church. You will do well to send them on their journey as befits God's service. For they have set out for his sake and have accepted nothing from the heathen. So we ought to support such men, that we may be fellow workers in the truth." The separate fraternal communities are here reminded of their mutual brotherliness (cf. 2 Jn 13) and warned against mutual exclusivity, but their being closed against the heathen is accepted, probably with some historical justification. Nevertheless, one senses that there is a danger here for the Christian idea of brotherhood. It has moved beyond the critical stage of indefiniteness, but threatens to become too fixed to lose that openness which it

[24] J. Michl in the Regensburg New Testament, 8, (Regensburg, 1953), 287.

must have from the very nature of the message of Christ.

THE IDEA OF BROTHERHOOD IN THE FATHERS

The name "brother" occurs frequently and as a matter of course in the Fathers up to the third century.[25] The theory of Christian brotherliness is developed in several directions, and material is taken over from the pagan environment. Thus it is baptism which is now regarded as the precise moment at which one becomes a "brother." It represents, as rebirth, the acceptance into the Christian "brotherhood" as the community calls itself.[26] In this rebirth the church is the mother, and God is the Father.[27] The connection of

[25] Schelkle, *op cit.*, 639 f. The usage is found in sepulchre symbolism until the fourth century (*see* H. Leclerq's article "Freres," *DACL*, V, 2, 2578–85 [esp. 2580 ff]).

[26] Tertullian, *De bapt.*, 20, 5 (*CCSL*, I, 295). For the community as *fraternitas*, *Ap.*, 39, 10 (*CCSL*, I, 151); *De praescr.*, 20, 8 (*CCSL*, I, 202); *De pud.*, 7, 22 (plural) (*CCSL*, II, 1294); *De virg vel.*, 14, 2 (*CCSL*, II, 1223). Since *De am.*, 48, 3 (*CCSL*, II, 854) and *Scorp.*, 8, 4 (*CCSL*, II, 1083), the three youths in the fiery furnace, can be described as *trina fraternitas*, Tertullian's idea of the church as the *corpus trium* could be in the background. See J. Ratzinger, *Volk und Haus Gottes*, 75 f.

[27] *De bapt.*, 20, 5 (*CCSL*, I, 295). On *mater ecclesia* and *fraternitas christianorum* in Cyprian, *see* Ratzinger, 87 ff. On the idea of *mater ecclesia* in general, *see* the plentiful material in H. Rahner, *Mater ecclesia* (Einsiedeln, 1944).

brotherhood and rebirth involves (perhaps at first unconsciously) a certain resemblance to the groups of the mystery religions, from which—as a further important formal element—the "secret discipline" is then taken over.[28] This necessarily meant a further closing of the ranks of the brotherhood in relation to others, toward which persecution doubtless contributed. On the other hand, it also made the inner cohesion into a truly living brotherhood. As the crux of Christian brotherhood we always recognize something which is the heart of the Christian "secret discipline" and, at the same time, the centre given by Jesus to his new people: the eucharistic meal of brotherhood.[29]

As the persecuted church was also—and remained—in the highest degree a missionizing church, we see, parallel with the limitation of the idea of brotherhood just described, a profound tendency toward delimitation. Ignatius of Antioch lays stress on a brotherly attitude toward one's persecutors. In imitation of their guiltless persecuted master, Christians must, by their

[28] See the article on "secret discipline" in *FAC*, I, 667–676 (O. Perler); *LTK*, I², 863 f. (O. Perler); *RGG*, I³, 606 ff. (J. Leipoldt).

[29] For the biblical aspect, *see* F. Kattenbusch, "Der Quellort der Kirchenidee," *Festgabe A. Harnack zum 70. Geburtstag* (Tubingen, 1921), 143–72; for the patristic, J. Ratzinger, *Volk und Haus Gottes;* for the systematic, J. Ratzinger, "Die Kirche als Geheimnis des Glaubens," *Lebendiges Zeugnis*, I (1956–7), 19–34.

kindness, show brotherliness toward their oppressors.[30] Tertullian also explicitly distinguishes the two kinds of brotherhood. One depends on common descent and embraces all men; the other depends on the common knowledge of God and the spirit of holiness that is drunk by Christians in common.[31] In his idea of brotherhood in general, Tertullian was probably influenced by Stoic ideas.[32]

By the third century, however, the word "brother" is found less and less as a designation among Christians. It is instructive for an understanding of the inner development of the church to see the two ways in which the word finally comes to be used. The first usage we find in Cyprian who no longer employs the word "brother" as a term of address to Christians, except to bishops and clerics.[33] This is no longer the old brotherhood of the faithful; it reminds one rather of the well-known secular idea of the brotherhood of princes with each other[34] which was later to become clearly apparent in the gradations of address for bishops,

---

[30] *Eph.*, 10, 3 (ed. J. A. Fischer, Darmstadt, 1956, 150).

[31] *Ap.*, 39, CCSL, I, 151 (Schelkle, *op. cit.*, 639).

[32] Schelkle, *op. cit.*, 640.

[33] Schelkle, *op. cit.*, 640: "It certainly sounds like a formula when Cyprian begins his epistles with '*fratres carissimi*.' In individual address he uses '*frater*' only for bishops and clerics; Cyprian calls only a confessor 'brother' (*Ep.*, 53)."

[34] See F. Dölger, "Brüderlichkeit der Fürsten," *RAC*, II, 641–6.

presbyters, and laymen. The other usage developed in the context of asceticism, in the monastic communities, in which the idea of "brother" and "sister" lived on after it had passed away from a church which had grown too vast for it to have any concrete meaning.[35] Thus there is a restriction of the idea of brotherhood to the hierarchy and to ascetics, to which actual church life had now become reduced. As we know, this state of affairs has persisted up to our own times, with all its inevitably damaging effects. Thus historical analysis has led to the point from which our reflection about the Christian idea of brotherhood today—its significance and its possibilities—must start.

[35] Schelkle, *op. cit.*, 640. See von Soden, *op. cit.*, 146, 24 ff.

AN ATTEMPT AT SYNTHESIS

Following this brief historical survey, let us now try to define the Christian idea of brotherhood. This Christian idea can be set out in the form of two different arguments, one of a dogmatic nature and one of a moral nature.

The basis of Christian brotherhood: faith

CHRISTIAN BROTHERHOOD, UNLIKE THE PURELY
SECULAR BROTHERHOOD OF MARXISM, IS, ABOVE
ALL, BROTHERHOOD BASED ON THE COMMON
PATERNITY OF GOD. UNLIKE THE IMPERSONAL
STOIC IDEA OF GOD THE FATHER AND THE VAGUE
PATERNAL IDEA OF THE ENLIGHTENMENT, THE
FATHERHOOD OF GOD IS A FATHERHOOD MEDIATED
BY THE SON AND INCLUDING BROTHERLY UNION
IN THE SON.

IF, THEREFORE, CHRISTIAN BROTHERHOOD IS TO
BE VITALLY REALIZED, BOTH A VITAL KNOWLEDGE
OF THE FATHERHOOD OF GOD AND A VITAL JOINING
WITH JESUS CHRIST IN A UNITY OF GRACE ARE
NECESSARY.

The fatherhood of God gives Christian brotherhood

its firm foundation. It is important here to understand fully the new knowledge that the Christian faith has given us of God's paternity. Mythical religion, Plato and the Stoics, and eighteenth-century deism all speak of God as a father. And yet it is something quite different when the Christian says "Our Father." Early mythical thought conceived of the sky as the world-creating force which, together with mother earth, produced all the life of the world. In this naturalistic sense, then, the sky can be called the "father" of men.[1] Greek philosophy spiritualized this idea without completely removing its basic assumption. In the eternal, transcendent idea of the good, Plato sees the father and the lord, but its quality as "person" remains in doubt, and there is no question of a personal relationship to the creatures of the world.[2] With the Stoics the return to naturalism is quite clear. Their doctrine of the fatherhood of God depends on a reinterpretation in terms of natural philosophy of the old myth of *hieros gamos* (sacred marriage) of Zeus and Hera. Thus it remains ultimately a proposition of natural philosophy when man appears in Epictetus as *idios huios tou theou* (God's own son).[3] It certainly does not mean that he is seen in relation to a personal, caring and loving,

[1] See G. Schrenk's article on *pater* (father) in *TWNT*, V, 951 f.
[2] See the texts quoted by Schrenk, *ibid.*, 954.
[3] *Diss.*, I, 19, 9; Schrenk, *ibid.*, 955, 28.

angry and forgiving, paternal God. He is merely the culminating point of the cosmos, the one most filled by its sublime powers. The uncosmic, strictly personalist idea of father, which gives to the paternity of God the seriousness of a true claim on us and to the fraternity of his children life and significance, is revealed only in the words of the bible and is thus apparent only to the eyes of faith. Insight into the brotherhood of men is given ultimately only to him who has seen, in faith, the full paternity of God.

At the same time the concreteness of God, his personal relation to man, also undergoes an increasing spiritualization in the language of Scripture—an increasing spiritualization which does not, however, lead to increasing rarification (as is always the danger), but, on the contrary, serves to intensify the concreteness and the living reality of his fatherhood. This God never becomes a God of the philosophers; he remains the living God, the God of Abraham, of Isaac and Jacob; more, he becomes the God of Jesus Christ and thus the God who has taken on our flesh and blood and our whole human nature. In Jesus Christ, God has not only spoken to men, but finally and radically made it possible for them to speak to him; for in him God became man and, as man, finally stepped out of his totally different being and entered into the dialogic situation of all men. Jesus the *man* stands as such within the community of discourse which unites all men as beings of the same order. The man Jesus can be addressed by every man, but in him it is God who is addressed. Thus the question of how changeable man can address a totally different, unchangeable God is resolved. In Christ, God has taken a piece of this world's time and of changeable creatureliness, drawn it to himself, and finally thrown open the door between him and his creatures. In Christ, God has become God more concretely, more personally, and more "addressably," "a partner of men." We are better placed to understand the importance of this for the Christian conception of fatherhood and brotherhood if we consider more closely the biblical growth of the idea. We have already seen that the Old Testament distinguishes two kinds of divine paternity and, correspondingly, two kinds of human childhood: the sonship of all peoples because of the creation; the sonship of Israel because of the election of Israel. The Old Testament expresses Israel's priority by (among other things) calling Israel the "firstborn son of God" (Ex 4:22).

At the time of the kings an important development takes place in Israel's understanding of herself. The king now became virtually the personification of all Israel; he represented, as it were, its "total person." (Since the research work by Pedersen, this expression of Max Scheler's can be used to describe Israelite thinking on this question.)[4] Thus the name "the son of God" is transferred to the king (2 Sam 7:14; Ps 2:7; 89:27). He is the son of God in the sense described, inasmuch as he represents Israel which has a special elective sonship in relation to God. When the idea of a king passed into the eschatological hope of salvation and the idea of the Messiah was formulated concretely, the title of sonship went with it and became an honorific designation for the king of the last times, the Messiah, as the fulfilled image of the true Israel. Exegesis of the last few decades has confirmed the view that nearly all the synoptic texts which call Jesus *huios tou theou* (Son of God) are not to be understood in the sense of a metaphysical statement about the eternal inner-trinitarian divine sonship of Jesus, but reproduce the messianic title of honor, designating him as the epitome of the true Israel.[5] This accords with the fact that Jesus saw himself expressly as the founder of a new Israel already founded in his person a conception that John expresses by having Jesus describe himself in two places in suggestive imagery as the new Jacob-Israel (1:51 [*cf.* Gen 28:12] and 4:6, 11–12).

---

[4] J. Pedersen, *Israel. Its Life and Culture*, I–II (London, 1946).

[5] *See*, for example, O. Cullmann, *The Christology of the New Testament* (London, 1959), 275–305. Concerning the disputed interpretation of Mk 14:61, *see* the controversy between Blinzler and Stauffer in *Hochland*, 49 (1956–7), 563–8.

If we compare these exegetical findings with our dogmatic acknowledgement of the divine sonship of Jesus, we can say that Christ is the fulfilment of what Israel only foreshadowed. He is truly the "Son." Thus he is ultimately the true and real Israel because he possesses the highest distinction of Israel, the sonship of God, in an infinitely more real way than was the case with the old people of God. At the same time, the fact that he has himself become a man, "Israel," shows that he does not regard his divine sonship as something reserved only for himself: the meaning of the incarnation is rather to make what is his available to all. Man can be "in Christ," enter into him, and become one with him; and whoever is in Jesus Christ shares his sonship and is able to say with him, "Abba," "my father."[6] The new Israel, which is composed of all the faithful, is no longer a son merely because of the choosing and summoning call of God, the ultimate concrete form of which is the Torah; she is a "son in the son" (Eckhart); she is a son through being planted in the innate Son of the Father (Jn 1:18), with whom we are *one single* body, one single "seed of Abraham." "You are all one in Christ Jesus," Paul emphasizes in Gal 3:28, after (in 3:16) he had emphasized that the promise given to

[6] According to Quell, *TWNT*, V, 984 f., *Abba* is, in fact, an expression that a child would use, almost like "daddy." In any case it expresses the reality of the new child-father relationship.

78

Abraham did not refer to many, but only to one man, Christ Jesus, with whom, however, we are united in the unity of a single man. Thus the ideas of fatherhood-sonship-brotherhood acquire a completely new ring, the ring of reality. Behind the word "father" there stands the *fact* of our true childhood in Christ Jesus (Gal 4:6; Rom 8:15 f.). What is new about the New Testament statements concerning the Father is not a new psychological atmosphere, nor a new subjective intensity, nor a new idea, but the new fact created by Christ. The mood of trusting love and pure devotion may be found in late Jewish prayers or in the texts of the Hermes mystery cult.[7] But in these it is ultimately *only* a question of atmosphere. What is expressed by them is valuable and profound, and can be largely taken over by the Christian. But it acquires in Christianity a new meaning by being founded firmly on fact —the fact of our real embodiment in Christ, which includes our becoming truly sons. What is true of the ideas of "fatherhood" and sonship" is no less true of "brotherhood." This is the foundamental dogmatic basis for the brotherliness of Christians among one another; for this brotherliness is founded on our being incorporated in Christ Jesus, in the uniqueness of a new man. Like the fatherhood of God, the brotherhood of Christians in the Lord is raised—through the Christ-

[7] Schrenk, *TWNT*, V, 957 ff.

event—above the realm of ideas to the dignity of true actuality. We also find here the concrete realization and the constant source of Christian brotherliness. It rests on the fact of our being embodied in Christ. The act that does this for us is baptism (which is renewed in penance). The celebration of the eucharist is the constant re-establishment of our bodily unity with the Lord and with one another. But with this idea we are already on the way toward realizing Christian brotherhood concretely, and that we shall pursue later on. Summing up what we have said so far, we can assert that Christian brotherhood differs from all other brotherhoods that transcend the sphere of blood brotherhood precisely in its character as real and actual. This is grasped in faith and acquired through the sacraments.

From these dogmatic conclusions we can deduce the Christian attitudes which are able to provide the basis for an ethos of true brotherhood. In general terms, these consist, as we have seen, in the conscious spiritual acceptance of the fatherhood of God and union with the life of Christ. We shall now endeavor to explore these two relationships a little further.

Christian brotherhood is ultimately founded on the faith that gives us our assurance of our real sonship in relation to the heavenly Father and of our brotherhood among one another. But here it is necessary to emphasize the social dimension of faith more than is generally done. To take only one example: when theologians today interpret the opening words of the Our Father, they usually restrict themselves to an analysis of the word "father," and this is in tune with our contemporary religious awareness. But a theologian such as Cyprian, on the other hand, chose to give speccial attention to the word "our."[8] In fact this word does have great importance, for only *one* man has the right to say *"my* Father" to God, and that is Jesus Christ, the only-begotten Son. All other men must say *"our* Father," for the Father is God for us only so long as we are part of the community of his children. For "me" he becomes a father only through my being in the "we" of his children. The Christian prayer to the Father "is not the call of a soul that knows nothing outside God and itself,"[9] but is bound to the community of our brothers, together with whom we make up the one Christ, in whom and through whom alone we are able to say "Father," because only through Christ and in Christ are we his "children." Thus, strictly speaking, we should not say that Christ taught men to call God "Father," but rather that it was he who taught them to say *"Our* Father"—and the "Our" is no less im-

---

[8] *De dom. or.*, 8, CSEL, III, 1 (Hartel), 271 f.; *see* Ratzinger, *Volk und Haus Gottes*, 99.

[9] Ratzinger, *ibid.*, 99.

portant than the "Father," for it *locates* faith and prayer, assigning them their Christological component. When we see this, Harnack's view[10] that the "Son" does not form part of the gospel proclaimed by Christ is shown to be obviously false. Its place is firmly fixed in the "our" and, in a logically developing *kerygma*, could not fail to emerge as the social dimension of faith. It is important that this social dimension should once more be brought to the consciousness of the faithful, that Christian belief in God the Father should be shown necessarily to involve the affirmation of our brothers, the brotherhood of all Christians.

Living faith in the spirit of the Our Father will necessarily lead to a new relationship to God and to our fellow man, whom we recognize as our brother. Toward God it includes the attitudes of trust and of love. God has accepted us as his children in Christ Jesus and thus has become our Father, and is the absolutely faithful and dependable God who has remained true to his covenant in spite of the sin of men —indeed, has been moved by this sin and faithlessness to an even greater outpouring of grace and forgiveness. He is the exact opposite of the Homeric "father of the gods and of men." This god is a domineering and unpredictable despot—and not despite his father-

[10] A. von Harnack, *What is Christianity?* (London, 1958⁵), 95 ff.

hood, but precisely because of it: there is a despotic quality in the Greek idea of fatherhood.[11] And yet this despotic father is not himself the highest power, for above, or beside him, stand *moira* (fate) and *themis* (the law of the cosmos), against which even he can do nothing.[12] Against this background the biblical idea of fatherhood acquires its true greatness. For this God is the ultimate power, power itself, *Pantocrator*, and, at the same time, the most reliable, unfailing fidelity. Both these qualities are able to move man to an ultimate, unshakable trust which is love and worship in one.

A second attitude which faith produces in us is in relation to our fellow men. One might call it, with Dietrich von Hildebrand, "the true loss of oneself."[13] To become a Christian means to become incorporated in the Son, in Christ, so that we become "sons in the Son." This is a sacramental, but also an ethical process. Its ethical nature is illuminated by a thought of Eckhart's which, when taken to its logical conclusion, is dogmatically incorrect but can still help us to see the present point more clearly. Eckhart interprets the dog-

[11] Schrenk, *TWNT*, V, 952 f.
[12] Schrenk, *op. cit.*, 952 f. *See* also J. Schmid, *Das Evangelium nach Matthaus*, 126.
[13] D. von Hildebrand, *Die Umbestaltung in Christus* (Einsiedeln, 1950), 326–38.

matic teaching that Christ possessed human nature, but not human personality, wrongly by saying that, in that case, Christ was "man in general," possessing humanity without any individuality or particular qualities. In one of his German sermons he expresses the doctrine of the two natures and the one person like this: "The eternal Word did not take upon himself this or that man, but rather did it take upon itself a free, undivided human nature."[14] This is an ethical reinterpretation of the doctrine of the hypostatic union. Eckhart seeks to make the dogmatic statement yield a basic ethical principle. For Christ is the goal of man, nay more: it is for man to be himself "in Christ," to grow into Christ. To the question of how man can grow into Christ, Eckhart's suggestion offers a surprisingly clear and simple answer. Christ is man, humanity free from any particular individuality. Accordingly, man grows into Christ the more that he becomes "man in himself"—the more that he loses himself, his own particular ego. What separates him from Christ is his own individuality, the

[14] The axiom *"assumpsit naturam,"* *Sermones de tempore*, VI, 2, 57, in Meister Eckhart, *Lateinische Werke*, IV (ed. Benz-Decker-Koch [Stuttgart, 1956]), 56 f. The quoted text from the 47th German sermon, 158, 1–3, can be found on p. 57, *n.* 1, together with a large number of further parallel texts. *See* also for the whole, J. Ratzinger, *Volk und Haus Gottes*, 234 ff. (esp. 235).

self-assertion of his ego. What unites him with Christ
is his general humanity. The measure of his share in the
hypostatic union, his being "in Christ," is the extent to
which he has destroyed his own ego; so that, according
to Eckhart, if he were able to rid himself entirely of
his ego, he would become identical with Christ. It is
not necessary here to enter on a discussion of this ethic,
which is an ethic of the mystical body of Christ and
yet runs the danger of turning into pure humanism.
The important thing here is to see the truth that lies
at the heart of it: to become one with Christ means to
lose one's "oneself," to cease to regard one's own ego
as an absolute. It is consistent with this basic view that
Eckhart's ethic has a marked social character and emphasizes the service of our neighbor rather than the joys
of contemplation.[15] The belief that we have all become
a single new man in Jesus Christ will always call us to
let the separating particularity of our own egos, the
self-assertion of human selfhood, melt into the community of the new man Jesus Christ. Whoever believes
in Jesus Christ has not only found an ethical model to
be imitated privately, but is called to break up his own

---

[15] For the social character of Eckhart's mysticism, *see* H. Piesch,
Meister Eckharts Ethik, (Lucerne, 1935), 111–122; and O. Karrer,
Meister Eckhart (Munich, 1926), 189–93.

merely private ego and merge into the unity of the body of Christ.

The ethic of Christ is essentially an ethic of the body of Christ. Inevitably, therefore, it means losing one's own ego and becoming one in brotherhood with all those who are in Christ. As an ethic of true self-loss, it necessarily includes the brotherhood of all Christians.

The removal of barriers within the brotherhood of Christians

UNION WITH CHRIST INCLUDES THE UNION OF
CHRISTIANS AMONG ONE ANOTHER, AND THUS
INVOLVES A REMOVAL OF THE SEPARATING
BARRIERS OF NATURE AND HISTORY. THEREFORE
THE ETHOS OF A BROTHERHOOD WITH EQUAL
RIGHTS MUST TRANSCEND THE NECESSARY
DIVISIONS OF CLASS OR HIERARCHIC ORDER.

The removal of barriers which had before seemed insurmountable is an essential part of the Christian experience of newness. "From now on, therefore, we regard no one from a human point of view; even though we once regarded Christ from a human point of view, we regard him thus no longer. Therefore, if any one is in Christ, he is a new creation; the old has passed away, behold, the new has come" (2 Cor 5:16–17). All previous differences lost their importance before the revolutionary reality of this new creation. The great unbridge-able difference which had divided the world now loses its meaning—the difference between Israel and the heathen, between pure and impure, between elect and non-elect.

> Remember that you were at that time separated from Christ, alienated from the commonwealth of Israel, and strangers to the covenant of promise, having no hope and without God in the world. But now in Christ Jesus you who once were afar off have been brought near in the blood of Christ. For he is our peace, who has made us both one, and has broken down the dividing wall of hostility, . . . that he might . . . reconcile us both to God in one body through the cross, thereby bringing the hostility to an end. And he came and preached peace to you who were far off and peace to those who were near. . . . [Eph 2:12–17; *cf.*, in this context, the vision of Peter before the baptism of Cornelius, Ac 10:9–16].

In Ephesians, the word "mystery" means specifically this miracle of the union of Jews *and* Gentiles in the one body of Christ.[1] The mystery of Christ is the

[1] G. Bornkamm's article on *mysterion* in *TWNT*, IV, 827. *See* H. Schlier's "Die Einheit der Kirche im Denken des Apostels Paulus," *Cath*, X, 1 (1954), 14–26; also his *Der Brief an die Epheser* (Dusseldorf, 1957), 61.

mystery of the removal of barriers. Other texts in Paul develop this idea: "For as many of you as were baptized into Christ have put on Christ. There is neither Jew nor Greek, there is neither slave nor free, there is neither male nor female; for you are all one in Christ Jesus," says Gal 3:27–8, placing the removal of the religious differences between Jew and Gentile side by side with that of the basic social differences between slave and free man, and between man and woman. We may note in this connection that, in contrast to the mystery religions, it is an exclusively Christian idea that "a 'sister' has the right to stand as an equal beside her 'brother.' "[2]

Colossians goes even further by including national barriers with the religious and social barriers that are removed by Christ. "Put on the new nature, which is being renewed in knowledge after the image of its creator. Here there cannot be Greek and Jew, circumcized and uncircumcized, barbarian, Scythian, slave, free man, but Christ is all, and in all" (Col 3:10–11). Before and above all these statements about the removal of barriers stand the inexorable words of the Lord to the rich young ruler: "Why do you call me good? No one is good but God alone" (Mk 10:18). They acknowledge only one true barrier: that between creator and creature. Before it all other differences become unimportant.

We recapture here the unique and irrevocable ex-

---

[2] Schelkle, *op. cit.*, 638.

perience of newness which is bound up with the early growth of Christianity and its overcoming of barriers. And yet the abiding actuality of what is said is also apparent in many ways. For example, the overcoming of nationalism is a task that every generation sets itself anew; and, in an age in which Europe is at last striving to break free from the internecine enmity of the past and achieve unity, it is becoming ever more important. It is equally apparent that our age no longer regards differences of class as ultimate, but seeks to remove them in a spirit of Christian brotherhood. Perhaps, however, it is valuable to consider in a little more detail one question which a Catholic in particular might ask himself in this connection: that of the ethos of hierarchic differences. None of the Pauline texts we have quoted refers to it, but we have the words of Christ (Mt 23:8–11):

> But you are not to be called rabbi, for you have one teacher, and you are all brethren. And call no man your father on earth, for you have one Father, who is in heaven. Neither be called masters, for you have one master, the Christ. He who is greatest among you shall be your servant. [*See* also the important text of Mt 20:25–8.]

If we take the preceding verses (1–8) as well, it is

clear that the false hierarchism and dignity of office cultivated by the Jews is contrasted with the undifferentiated brotherliness of Christians. And one cannot avoid the serious challenge that this text puts to us: Does not our actual Christian reality resemble more the Jewish hierarchism castigated by Jesus than the picture he gave of Christian brotherhood? In his book on apostleship, Schelkle takes up a point from this text and says:

> Thus the Lord's saying takes exception to any man's being addressed in the Church as father in spirit. And if the saying is preserved in the gospel, then this probably really proves that the church of that time did not award the title "father" to anyone but God. . . . Granted that by the testimony of their writings Paul and other apostles feel like fathers of the faithful, granted too that the expression became a regular form of address and exists as such even today, . . . still, such a practice always finds its meaning its value, indeed its limitation, in Mt 23:9. May a man claim to be related to another in spiritual paternity or maternity? Do not such right and such honour really belong to God alone . . . ?[3]

[3] K. H. Schelkle, *Discipleship and Priesthood* (London, 1966), 44 f.

One is obliged to add that not only the title of "father" is qualified by this text, but the whole *external* (and I mean *external*) form of hierarchism that has developed over the centuries.

There are a few further observations that might be made. The New Testament clearly differentiates the authorized representative who continues the mission of Jesus in an official capacity from the ordinary believers who are not so authorized.[4] What we call "the hierarchy" and "the priesthood" are New Testament realities. A Catholic theologian will need to lay great emphasis on this, but he has no reason to conceal the fact that the New Testament has its own particular verbal usage. It never calls the officials "priests," or the office "office." The Greek words for office (*arkhe, exousia, time, telos*) are not, for the New Testament, appropriate descriptions for the offices of the church.

The New Testament knows these words, but does not employ them in the realm of the Church; rather it draws on the word *diakonia*. *Arkhe* is restricted in New Testament usage to the authority

---

[4] Of the vast literature on the question of office in the church, let us mention here an impressive Protestant publication which shows its authorized representative character as based on the New Testament: O. Linton, "Kirche und Amt im Neuen Testament," *Ein Buch von der Kirche*, ed. Aulén-Fridrichsen-Nygren and others (Göttingen, 1951), 110–44.

of synagogue and a state or to the angelic powers. *time* to the dignity of office of the Old Testament highpriest. The result of such lexicographical investigation is impressive enough evidence that office in the Church is an institution essentially ordered to service. The result also makes manifest the self-understanding of the New Testament that order and law mean essentially different things in the Church and in the world. Therefore they cannot be named with the same words.[5]

This final statement is central. One can in no way identify the New Testament office, which is in fact New Testament service, with the phenomenon of priesthood in other religions. It is by nature something totally different. That it resembles priesthood factually, purely as a phenomenon, does not derive from its nature, but from the fact that a perfect fulfillment of being in the world of concrete appearances always remains impossible. It comes from a breaking-in of the individual element which is not of Christ. So it is that, to this day, the sixth sacrament is called, in the language of the Church, not *sacerdotium*, but *ordo*.

There is a further historical point to be made. The special character of the Christian office emerges with particular clarity when we compare the Christian apostle

[5] Schelkle, *Discipleship*, 39*n*.

93

with his direct parallels in the history of religion, the rabbi and the *theios anthropos* ("man of God") of the Greeks. Both the latter have their own authority, whereas the essential thing for an apostle is to be a servant of Christ and, like Christ, to live by the motto, "My teaching is not mine, but his who sent me" (Jn 7:16).[6] Thus the sense of mission for the rabbi and the "man of God" is an awareness of self; for the apostle it is an awareness of service. "The rabbi's pupil has the goal of becoming a master himself. But for Jesus' disciple, discipleship is not a beginning; it is the fulfilment and destination of his life. He always remains a disciple."[7]

We might add that, as a "father," he still remains a "brother"; his fatherly office is a form of brotherly service, and nothing else. We are here at the point from which we can see the positive element in the Protestant understanding of Christianity, such as we find in Bultmann and in the whole "theology of crisis" preceding him. We can agree here with E. Wolf in the closing sentence of his article on the historical development of Christianity:

[6] *See* K. H. Rengstorf's article on *apostolos* in *TWNT*, I, 406–16 (esp. 408 ff.); and Schelkle, *Discipleship*, 24 f. For Jn 7:16 *see* the splendid exegesis of it by Augustine, *Tr. in Joh.*, XXIX, 3–5, *CCSL*, 36, 285 f.

[7] Schelkle, *Discipleship*, 24.

Christianity is ultimately not a cultural achievement, or an ideology, or the solution of the problems of humanity, or even in its essence "religion," but rather the crisis of all religions in Christ.[8]

[8] *RGG*, I, 1705.

This is an element in Christianity that cannot be lightly set aside. By removing all barriers it continually places the actual differentiations within the church within this crisis, compelling us to purify them ever anew from within and fill them with the spirit of the same brotherhood that made us "all one in Christ Jesus" (Gal. 3:28).

The *limits*
of the *brotherly community*

CHRISTIANITY DOES NOT MEAN THE REMOVAL OF
ALL BARRIERS, BUT ITSELF CREATES A NEW
BARRIER, THAT BETWEEN CHRISTIANS AND
NON-CHRISTIANS. CONSEQUENTLY THE
CHRISTIAN IS THE BROTHER OF HIS FELLOW
CHRISTIAN, BUT NOT OF THE NON-CHRISTIAN.
HIS COMMITMENT TO LOVE IS
INDEPENDENT OF THIS, HOWEVER, AND IS
DIRECTED TOWARD ANYONE IN NEED WHOM HE
CAN HELP. NEVERTHELESS THE BUILDING UP AND
CULTIVATION OF A VITAL INNER CHRISTIAN
BROTHERHOOD REMAINS ONE OF HIS CHIEF
CONCERNS.

Here we come upon a decisive difference between the
Catholic and the Protestant understandings of Christian-

ity. That Christianity has in fact created a limited religious community separate from other groups—the church—is clear. The question is: How long has this limitation existed, and how legitimate is it?[1] The first question has already been answered in our historical analysis in which we found that as early as Paul there was already a clear differentiation of the Christian communities and that an inner-Christian ethos had developed. The second question—the question of its legitimacy—is more or less identical with the basic question of how the Catholic idea of the church is to be justified, and that question cannot be treated here in full. Nevertheless, in our analysis of the ethos of brotherhood among the early Christians we shall see that it is based on the assumption of a closed brotherly community. Hence the nature of this ethos is important for our knowledge of the self-understanding of early Christianity. Finally, we must not forget that Jesus himself did not describe everyone as his brothers and sisters, but only those who

[1] We can merely mention here the interesting new formulation of these much-discussed questions by W. Kamlah, *Christentum und Geschichtlichkeit. Untersuchungen zur Entstehung des Christentums und zu Augustins "Burgerschaft Gottes"* (Stuttgart, 1951). Naturally there is no suggestion that Protestant theologians have only one view on this subject—the variety of their positions is well known—but an "eschatological," anti-institutional view of the church is widely held by Protestants today, and is rooted in their fundamental religious attitude.

were one with him in their assent to the will of the
Father (Mk 3:33–4). Only in the parable of the last
judgment (Mt 25:31–46) is the idea of brotherhood
separated from the idea of unity in the will of the Lord
and applied to all those in need, for these are called
brothers of the Son of Man who governs the world (but
not automatically brothers of believers). But even that
is not a judgment on them so much as on the claim each
of them has on the love of Christians. With the choosing
of the twelve, the patriarchs of the new Israel, to whom
Jesus gives the name "brothers," a special, separate community had already in fact been created.

Let us also remember that Jesus has predicted to his
disciples the collapse and failure of all earthly brotherhood and family love: "Brother will deliver up brother
to death, and the father his child, and children will rise
against parents and have them put to death" (Mt
10:–21). But he had also promised them, in the midst
of all persecution, a new brotherly community in this
world (Mk 10:30). His disciples were not to remain
homeless even in this world and in spite of their re-
nunciation of all earthly habitation. The brotherhood
of all Christians was coming.

Thus it is only Christians who are true brothers—the
others are called *hoi exo*, those who stand outside (1
Thes 4:10–12; cf. 1 Cor 5:12, 13; Col 4:5).[2] Only this

---

[2] See Sladeczek, *op. cit.*, 273 and 291.

limited application of the idea of brotherhood is Christian; removal of this barrier was an essentially unrealizable ideal of the Enlightenment. Only within this limitation is the idea of brotherhood a practical possibility. Again the critical question arises: Is it realizable, even so? Or are the borders too widely drawn? Is not the Church too large, too vast for it to be a true community of brothers?

Here we must go back to the original Christian meaning of *ekklēsia*, which at first meant the actual realization within the particular local community of the one Church.[3] Brotherhood can first be realized only within the local community—within the particular parish. Heinz Schürmann has pointed out that the question of the size of the parish community ought to be governed by this. It should be possible for everyone to know everyone else. "For you cannot live in brotherhood with someone that you don't even know."[4] One may go on to ask how the brotherhood of parishioners can be achieved in practice. Again a consideration of the original meaning of *ekklesia* can help us. The word not only means "church" and "local community," but it

---

[3] See K. L. Schmidt's article on *ekklesia* in *TWNT*, III, 503 ff.; F. Kattenbusch, "Der Quellort der Kirchenidee," 170–2; A. Wikenhauser, *Die Kirche als der mystische Leib Christi nach dem Apostel Paulus*, (Munster, 1937), 4–13.

[4] *Gemeinde als Bruderschaft*, 23.

can also mean "religious assembly." These three meanings are not simply distinct, unrelated to each other, but are, in fact, much more three levels of a single meaning and, consequently, often shade into one another. They are connected in the following way: the one Church always exists concretely in the concrete local community. The local community realizes itself as the Church in the religious assembly, that is, above all in the celebration of the eucharist.[5] Consequently Christian brotherhood demands concretely the brotherhood of the individual parish community. This brotherhood has its source and centre in the celebration of the eucharistic mysteries. In fact, in the classical theology of the Church, the Eucharist has been seen not so much as the soul's meeting with Christ, but rather as the *concorporatio cum Christo*—as the Christians' becoming one in the one body of the Lord.[6] A celebration of the Eucharist that is to be the source of brotherhood must both be inwardly recognized and performed as a sacrament of brotherhood and also externally appear to be such. The recognition that *ekklesia* (church) and *adelphotes* (brotherhood) are the same thing, that the

[5] Kattenbusch, *op. cit.*, 170 ff. *See* also Wikenhauser, 11 ff.
[6] This is developed in J. Ratzinger, *Volk und Haus Gottes*. *See* also F. Hofmann, "Glaubensgrundlagen der liturgischen Erneuerung," *Fragen der Theologie heute*, ed. Feiner-Trutsch-Bockle (Einsiedeln, 1957), 487–517.

Church that fulfills itself in the celebration of the Eucharist is essentially a community of brothers, compels us to celebrate the Eucharist as a rite of brotherhood in responsory dialogue—and not to have a lonely hierarchy facing a group of laymen each one of whom is shut off in his own missal or other devotional book. The Eucharist must again become visibly the sacrament of brotherhood in order to be able to achieve its full, community-creating power. This does not imply a social dogmatism: the vocation of the individual Christian can often be fulfilled quietly in a life of retirement. But even a vocation like this is a form of brotherly service and, therefore, far from invalidating the brotherly nature of the community rite of the Church, further confirms it.

Consideration of the Eucharist takes us a step farther, too. Its celebration originally comprised, of course, both the liturgical meal and an ordinary, "physical" meal shared by Christians meeting together in one large unit.[7] The liturgy and ordinary living had not yet become separated. This situation cannot be reconstructed under present circumstances, but Schürmann rightly points out that the need still remains for parishes to develop appropriate forms of community life outside the liturgy in order to supplement the liturgical coming-together

[7] H. Schurmann's "Die Gestalt der urchristlichen Eucharistiefeier," *MTZ*, 6 (1955), 107–31, and the literature listed there.

and make possible direct brotherly contact.[8] These forms will vary according to circumstances, but we may make one general point: inasmuch as brotherhood in the parish is, as it were, divided up among different societies or organizations, it is necessary to keep bringing people together in larger groups in order to emphasize their relationship to the greater unity of the parish. The individual organization is justified only insofar as it serves the brotherhood of the whole community. This aim of making the parish community a true brotherhood ought to be taken very seriously. Today a trade union or a party can exist as a live and fraternal community, and so the actual experience of brotherhood for all the Christian members of a parish community can and, therefore, should become a primary goal. It would be a universal experience which transcended all barriers, of course, for in every parish there are men of different professions and often of different languages and nationalities. It is this universality which gives the parish a superior position to an organzation based on any other community of interests. And the parishes ought to come to see one another as sisters, according to the words of John's second Epistle (5:13)—sisters who, in the fellowship of their faith and love, build up together the great unity of the mother Church, the body of the Lord.

[8] *Gemeinde als Bruderschaft,* 24 f.

A final question deserves attention: that of the relationship of the Christian community to those outside it. To begin with, it can do no harm to underline once again that this "outside" does indeed exist—that there really are people who are not brothers or not yet brothers. On this point we are always inclined to think more in rationalist eighteenth-century terms than in Pauline and Christian terms; and so we tend to dislike any line of demarcation. In fact, however, the Christian line of demarcation ultimately serves a universal openness, as we shall see. There must, first of all, be a limitation, the formation of a definite, tangible brotherly community which raises the whole from empty romanticism to the level of concrete realizability. Thus it is understandable that Paul's prescriptions for the relationship toward "outsiders" are in part open, but also in part definitive of the frontier. They are open when Paul demands total serving love toward anyone who approaches a Christian and needs his help (Rom 13:8; 1 Thess 3:12; 5:15; Ti 3:2; also 1 Cor 9:19),[9] when the Christian is told to pray for all men (1 Tim 2:1), to respect non-Christian authority (Rom 13:1 ff.; Ti 3:1; cf. 1 Tim 6:1, 2; Ti 2:9; Eph 6:5; Col 3:22 ff.; 1 Pt 2:13–18), and to show himself by his whole being a

[9] For the whole subject, *see* the careful research of Sladeczek, *op. cit.*, 288–95, where every statement by St Paul about the Christian attitude to *hoi exo* is collected and tabulated. I am indebted to Sladeczek for this whole section.

true benefactor of the world (Phil 2:15 ff.; Rom 12:17;
2 Cor 8:21; 1 Thess 4:12; 5:22; Rom 15:2; 1 Tim
4:12). Above all, Paul does not see it as any part of his
business and, hence, of any Christian's "to sit in judgment on the moral state and the eternal lot of those
who are outside the church community. 'For what have
I to do with judging outsiders? . . . God judges those
outside' (1 Cor 5:12, 13)."[10] Behind this attitude of
respect for the spiritual integrity of a non-Christian
there is also a sense of keeping within proper bounds.
It is expressed more explicitly in Col 4:5: "conduct
yourselves wisely towards outsiders."

This wisdom will also dictate caution lest the
Christian in self-surrender for the good of the
world may himself fall away from his life in
God. . . . Again and again the Christian must re-
mind himself of his basic opposition to the world
and honestly answer, in every specific situation, the
question: "What has a believer in common with
an unbeliever?" (2 Cor 6:15). Apart from the
correct fulfilment of duty toward all, and apart
from the showing of love toward our neighbors, . . .
the Christian must seek no share or fellowship with
unbelievers.[11]

[10] Sladeczek, *op. cit.*, 292.
[11] Sladeczek, *op. cit.*, 293 f.

For this reason Christians must strive for the greatest possible independence from non-Christians[12] and not choose them for their habitual companions.[13] In fact, they should have as little as possible to do with them (2 Cor 6.17).[14]

In attempting to transfer such statements from their original setting into the present, we are faced with the difficult question of where the frontier of Christian brotherhood is today. Does the brotherly community of the parish consist of all those who are baptized and are registered officially as Catholics, or can one call true brothers only the practicing Catholics? This question is difficult to answer because it has no direct analogy in Paul, and the existence of non-believing Christians on the scale of the present day was at that time unknown. And yet the situation did arise. Paul coined

[12] Sladeczek, *op. cit.*, 294, points 7 and 8. He shows here that, according to Eph 4:28; 1 Thes 4:11; 2 Thes 3:12, the Christian should care for his own bodily needs and reduce them to the essential so that he does not have to approach someone outside (1 Thes 4:12). The text 1 Cor 7:23 ("do not become *douloi ton anthropon*") Sladeczek interprets from 1 Cor 7:21 (*ei kai dunasai eleutheros genesthai, mallon khresai*) and 1 Cor 3:3, 4 (a synonymous use of *anthropos* and *sarkikos*) as meaning that Christians should not place themselves at the service of non-Christians. The warning of 2 Cor 6:14 could mean that Christians should not have any common business with unbelievers.

[13] Sladeczek, *op. cit.*, 294, no. 9: Eph 5:6–7.

[14] Further texts in Sladeczek, *op. cit.*, 294 f.

the word *pseudadelphos* to describe it.[15] If one ignores the pejorative element in the term and, in accordance with what we have said above, refrains from judging the conscience of the other, then one may say that this is the Pauline category for the non-believing Christian. Concerning the position of such people to Christ, and thus to the community, St. Paul says, "Any one who does not have the Spirit of Christ does not belong to him" (Rom 8:9).

This would appear to justify the view that it is only participation in the eucharistic liturgical assembly that makes a person a true member of the Christian fraternal community. If a man never takes part in the brotherly meal of Christians, he cannot be considered as belonging to the brotherhood. The brotherly community of the Christians consists of those, and only those, who come with at least a certain regularity to share in the eucharistic celebration. Only this definition is Pauline, and only this definition is realistic. For only on this view can we hope, with any justification, for an actual realization of a conscious brotherly community. This does not mean, of course, that we should write off those

[15] Schelkle, *RAC*, I, 638. There is a thorough analysis of the idea in Sladeczek, *op. cit.*, 279–88 (particularly 279–81). If one wanted to apply the word in the sense suggested to the present situation, one could probably best translate it as "Christian in name only."

who have been baptized but who have lost the living faith and, therefore, any direct sharing in Christian brotherhood. On the contrary, it means that we must rid ourselves of a dangerous illusion that can easily prevent us from recognizing the true measure of our responsibility toward those whose brothers we could be, but unfortunately all too little are. Moreover, the relation of those who are Christians in name only (*pseudadelphoi*) to the Christian fraternal community is different from that of those totally outside it. Paul exhorts Christians to practice truth and kindness toward them in teaching and preaching,[16] to continue to show them the light of the Word. Only when this is fruitless does he advise breaking off relations with them, keeping out of their way (1 Tim 6:5; 2 Cor 6:17; Rom 16:17; 1 Cor 5:9, 11; 2 Thess 3:14; 2 Tim 3:5; Ti 3:10; 2 Thess 3:14), and even in extreme cases excluding them formally from the community (1 Cor 5:13). But the goal always remains that their hearts should be changed and that they should be brought back fully into the brotherly community of Christians (2 Cor 2:6–11).[17]

[16] Sladeczek, *op. cit.*, 281–6.
[17] Sladeczek, *op. cit.*, 286 ff.

True universalism

THE SEPARATING-OFF OF THE LIMITED CHRISTIAN
BROTHERHOOD IS NOT THE CREATION OF SOME
ESOTERIC CIRCLE, BUT IS INTENDED TO SERVE THE
WHOLE. THE CHRISTIAN BROTHERLY COMMUNITY
DOES NOT STAND AGAINST THE WHOLE, BUT FOR IT.
THE BROTHERHOOD OF CHRISTIANS FULFILS ITS
RESPONSIBILITY FOR THE WHOLE THROUGH
MISSIONIZING, THROUGH AGAPE, AND THROUGH
SUFFERING.

If the foundation of the Church, and thus the realization
of Christ's mission, has created a new duality among
men—that of the Church and the non-Church—then it
is clear that the real goal of the work of Jesus refers
not to the part, but to the whole—to total humanity.[1]
This healing of the whole takes place, according to the

[1] This is particularly clear in Rom 5:12–21. *See* the *polloi* of
Mk 10:45 par. and Mk 14:24 par.

will of God, in the dialectical antithesis of the few and the many, in which the few are the starting point from which God seeks to save the many. This basic connection has never been so clearly expressed as in the election doctrine of Karl Barth, whose basic ideas we shall briefly summarize here.[2]

Barth's primary insight is that election has to be understood Christologically—in terms of salvation history. It is not an event which takes place between a terrifying divine absolute on the one side and an isolated creature on the other, but one which in every case passes concretely through Christ. Whereas a theory of election that disregards this must operate with two unknowns—God and man—in Christ the two unknowns become known. For in Christ what God is—he is grace—becomes visible; at the same time, what man is—he who experiences grace which releases him from guilt—also becomes visible. This becomes even clearer in the historical mission of Christ. Jesus Christ, himself innocent, is chosen to expiate the guilt of the world and in this sense to be the object of divine rejection, that is, to bear the fate of rejection which otherwise

[2] Karl Barth, *Church Dogmatics*, 2, 2, (Edinburgh, 1958). The following paragraphs are indebted to H. U. von Balthasar, *Karl Barth* (Cologne, 1951), 186–201. As we are not concerned here with an exegesis of Barth himself, I have merely drawn out the appropriate lines of his thinking and related them to our present problem.

would befall all other men. Thus the predestination of Christ is in quite a new sense *praedestinatio gemina*. This expression, originally coined by Gottschalk and taken up again by Calvin, meant for the latter the division of mankind, a twofold predestination—that to salvation, and that to damnation. Barth takes this idea of Calvin's and transforms it. For Jesus Christ, the only one worthy of salvation, now takes its complete opposite, the *whole* of damnation, on himself in a sacred exchange.

> In the election of Jesus Christ, which is the eternal will of God, God has ascribed to man the former, election, salvation and life; and to Himself He has ascribed the latter, reprobation, perdition and death.[3]

In other words, in the normal course of events God must damn the sinner and elect the just man; in Christ, however, there takes place the paradoxical miracle of grace which reverses this: he who alone is just and thus alone is chosen (because the only one worthy), Christ, becomes rejected, takes the fate of the rejection of all upon himself, and thus renders all in his place—in him and through him—elected, just as he had become rejected in us and through us. *Praedestinatio gemina* no

[3] Barth, *op. cit.*, 2, 2, 187. *See* also Balthasar, *op. cit.*, 189.

longer means, as in Calvin and perhaps even in Gottschalk, that a part of humanity is predestined to happi-
ness and the other to damnation; it means, rather, that
God passes the sentence of damnation on himself in
Christ and thus makes free for us the place of election,
to which then, through our salvation, Christ himself
also returns. The will of God in election is therefore
double, but not twofold.[4]

From this point we can take a further step which
brings us back to our theme. What took place with
Jesus Christ, the exchange in the history of election, is
not limited to him alone, but is reflected, according to
Barth, in the history of creation (in the dualities of light
and darkness, earth and water—a somewhat doubtful
theory), and is seen, above all, in salvation history.

> The election of one is always the non-election
> of another. But the one elected is always chosen
> for the sake of the one not chosen, and has to bear
> the burden of his non-election vicariously, so that
> in fact he who is not chosen is the chosen one,
> and the one chosen is he who is not chosen.[5]

Barth rightly points out the great antithetical pairs of
salvation history whom we encountered when we were

---

[4] Barth, *op. cit.*, 2, 2, 171.
[5] Balthasar, *op. cit.*, 191.

analyzing the Old Testament idea of brotherhood: Cain and Abel, Ishmael and Isaac, Esau and Jacob.[6] The history of these pairs of brothers has only a provisional ending in the rejection of one and the election of the other. Jesus' parable of the prodigal son, which might perhaps be better called his parable of the two brothers, and the doctrine of the two peoples that Paul develops in Rom 9–11, bring about the great reversal: rejection now in the last analysis leads directly to election—the rejected man is now chosen in his very rejection.

> They are quite different, and yet both have their true existence in him [Christ]. In him, who was originally both, chosen and rejected, their opposition to each other is seen as necessary. And in him too is grounded not only the relativity of their opposition, but also the fact of their being, in their antithesis, brothers. . . . Just as the election of Jesus Christ has its meaning in his vicarious rejection, and just as, vice versa, his vicarious rejection is the confirmation of his election, the elected and

[6] Balthasar, *op. cit.*, 196. (Barth also mentions a number of other pairs who are not, however, so important: Saul and David, the two prophets of 1 Kgs 13, the two robbers on the cross, and Judas and Paul. He crowns the whole with an interpretation of the relationship between synagogue and church. *See* also H. Fries, "Kirche als Ereignis. Zu Karl Barths Lehre von der Kirche," *Cath*, 11, 2 [1958], 81–107.)

the rejected do not stand opposed to each other, but next to and for each other.[7]

In other words, the mystery of this vicariousness, given in Christ and forming the basis of all election, is continued out from Christ according to the will of God in a whole system of vicarious relationships throughout salvation history as its fundamental law. Just as Christ, the chosen one, became in a sacred exchange the one rejected for us in order to confer on us his election, this exchange relationship recurs constantly in salvation history following him. Again and again he who is chosen, called by grace to the knowledge of faith and of love, must be ready to be vicariously rejected, so that through him another can be chosen also. One stands in the place of the other, and it is an expression of God's faith in us that he draws us into this system of vicarious election.

This takes us a step further. Ultimately this system cannot be based on individuals alone, but finds its comprehensive framework in the antithesis of Church and non-Church, of *laos* and *oulaos*. The Church, as such and as a whole, is the bearer of this vicarious election, the highest mission of which is to become vicarious rejection. The task of the Church and of the individual Christian is a dynamic one. Just as the individual who is chosen can never cut himself off from those whom

[7] Balthasar, *op. cit.*, 194.

he thinks are not, so the Church, as a chosen community, cannot cut itself off from those who are not God's people. Election is always, at bottom, election for others. For the Church as for the individual, election is identical with the missionary obligation. The Church is, therefore, "an open area, a dynamic concept; for all its visibility, the Church is only the movement of the kingdom of God into the world in the sense of an eschatological totality."[8] In relation to Christian brotherhood this means that, however important it is for the Church to grow into the unity of a single brotherhood, it must always remember that it is only one of two sons, one brother beside another, and that its mission is not to condemn the wayward brother, but to save him. The Church, it is true, must unify itself to form a strong inner brotherhood in order to be truly *one* brother. But it does not seek to be *one* brother in order finally to shut itself off from the other; rather it seeks to be one brother because only in this way can it fulfill its task toward the other, living for whom is the deepest meaning of its existence, which itself is grounded wholly in the vicarious existence of Jesus Christ.

And so at last we arrive at the Christian answer to the question of the idea of brotherhood raised at the beginning: the problem of the two zones of ethical behavior. In contrast to the Stoics and the Enlightenment,

[8] Balthasar, 197.

Christianity affirms the existence of the two different zones and calls only fellow believers "brothers." On the other hand, however, Christianity, unlike the mystery cults, is wholly free of a desire to form some self-sufficient esoteric group. Rather the separating-off of some has its ultimate significance only in the service it fulfills for the others who are, at bottom, the "other brother" and whose fate is in the hands of the first brother. We can therefore be certain that the Church will gain in missionary power as it begins to make its own internal brotherliness more vital.[9]

There remains the task of defining more closely the concrete, day-to-day manner of Christian service towards the "other" brother. The first obligation laid on a Christian is that of missionizing, and here again there is a certain dialectic which needs to be taken seriously. On the one hand stands the public commission of Christ: "What I tell you in the dark, utter in the light; and what you hear whispered, proclaim upon the housetops" (Mt 10:27). This is completed in the mis-

---

[9] For the Christian, every man is ultimately a "brother," either as the "other brother" or as he with whom we are joined together in the unity of the "one brother." Apart from the primarily Christological basis of this double brotherhood, the common fatherhood of God, of course, still stands in the background.

sionary command, "Go therefore and make disciples of all nations" (Mt 28:19), and corresponds to the public nature of Christ's own teaching: "I have spoken openly to the world; I have always taught in synagogues and in the temple, where all Jews come together; I have said nothing secretly" (Jn 18:20; *cf.* Mk 14:49). On the other hand there is the saying of Christ which became the basis of the secret discipline of the early Christians: "Do not give dogs what is holy; and do not throw your pearls before swine, lest they trample them under foot and turn to attack you" (Mt 7:6). This is in accord with a certain reserve in Christ's teaching: "To you has been given the secret of the kingdom of God, but for those outside everything is in parables" (Mk 4:11). The problem hereby posed need not be pursued here in detail. The main point is that it is the role of the Church to speak to the world the word of God given in Christ, to witness publicly before the world to the public salvation work of God so that everyone can hear it. At the same time, however, it must perform this task with a holy discretion. It must not try to catch men with the word unawares, as it were, without their knowing it. It has no right to draw the word out of a hat, like a conjuror. And it must recognize that there are places where the word would be wasted, thrown away, if it were spoken. These considerations are important for the question of Church propaganda, as for example in religious broadcasting on radio and television.[10] He best disseminates the word who does not squander it (for what is too cheap or too easy is reckoned of little value), but proclaims it.

The second obligation of the Christian toward the non-Christian is *agape*. This takes two forms: first, the relations of Christians among one another ought to have an attractive and exemplary force, constituting an effective active mission. They should make Christians a "lamp on a stand" (Mk 4:21), a "city set on a hill" (Mt 5:14). "In the midst of a crooked and perverse generation" Christians are to "shine as lights in the world" (Phil 2:15). But all that is not enough. For these words of the Lord are meant for Christians too: "And if you salute only your brethren, what more are you doing than others? Do not even the Gentiles do the same?" (Mt 5:47). Christians can never, and must never, be satisfied with saluting and loving their brothers, that is, their fellow believers; they must follow the Lord who performed his work of love for those who neither knew nor loved him (*see* Rom 5:6), direct-

[10] For the discussion which arose some years ago on the theme of the Mass on television, see the full survey of the literature in the *HK*, VII (1952–3), 518–20, with references to the positions of Volk, Pieper, and Guardini who were opposed to it as, for other reasons, was K. Rahner, "The Mass and Television," *Mission and Grace*, I (London, 1963), 255–75.

ing their love to all those who need them, and without asking for thanks or a response. Everyone who needs their help is, by virtue of that, and independently of his own belief, a brother of Christ—in fact, a manifestation of the Lord himself (Mt 25:31–46). A true *parousia* of Christ takes place wherever a man recognizes and affirms the claim on his love that goes out from a fellow man in need.

The last and highest mission of the Christian in relation to non-believers is to suffer for them and in their place as the Master did. At the end of his life, only a few days before his passion, Christ described his life's mission in these words: "The Son of man also came not to be served but to serve, and to give his love as a ransom for many" (Mk 10:45). These words express not only the basic law of Christ's own life, but the basic law of all Christian discipleship. The disciples of Christ will always be "few," as the Lord said, and as such stand before the mass, the "many," as Jesus, the one, stands before the many (that is, the whole of mankind). "For the gate is narrow, and the way is hard that leads to life, and those who find it are few" (Mt 7:14; *cf. v.* 13: the "many" are those who go by the easy way to destruction). "The laborers are few" (Mt 9:37). "Few are chosen" (Mt 22:14, in contrast to the "many" called). "Fear not, little flock" (Lk 12:32). "Behold, I send you out as sheep in the midst of wolves" (Mt

10:16). The disciples of Jesus are few, but as Jesus himself was one "for the many," so it will always be their mission to be not against, but "for the many." When all other ways fail, there will always remain the royal way of vicarious suffering by the side of the Lord. It is in its defeat that the Church constantly achieves its highest victory and stands nearest to Christ. It is when it is called to suffer for others that it achieves its highest mission: the exchange of fate with the wayward brother, and thus his secret restoration to full sonship and full brotherhood. Seen in this way, the relationship between the "few" and the "many" reveals the true measure of the Church's catholicity. In external numbers it will never be fully "catholic" (that is, all-embracing), but will always remain a small flock—smaller even than statistics suggest, statistics which lie when they call many "brothers" who are in fact merely *pseudadelphoi*, Christians by name only. In its suffering and love, however, it will always stand for the "many," for all. In its love and its suffering it surmounts all frontiers and is truly "catholic."

POSTSCRIPT

This discussion of the problem of Christian brotherhood has endeavored to apply what the New Testament says to the world today, even where what it says seems unexpected, even alien, to us. As I followed up the references, sometimes with surprise, in my mind there arose the question of the "separated brethren," the popular designation of Christians of differing confessions who thus express, across the gulf of their separation, their common adherence in faith to Jesus Christ, their brother. Must this formula be discarded because the New Testament restricts brotherhood, in the narrower sense, to those who share the one table, united through their common communion, which cannot exist among separated Christians? But then, what is the relation of these Christians to one another? Is the non-Catholic Christian, for a Catholic, the "other" brother only in the sense in which an unbaptized person is? Or does the community of baptism and the confession of the one Lord not, in fact, impart to him a greater share of fellowship? It is not easy to answer such questions, especially as they have seldom been asked in a sufficiently radical way, for fear of touching wounds that are still open. And yet it is necessary to ask this, just as truth is necessary for love.

The difficulty in the way of giving an answer is a profound one. Ultimately it is due to the fact that there is no appropriate category in Catholic thought for the phenomenon of Protestantism today (one could say the same of the relationship to the separated Churches of the East). It is obvious that the old category of "heresy" is no longer of any value. Heresy, for Scripture and the early Church, includes the idea of a personal decision against the unity of the Church, and heresy's characteristic is *pertinacia*, the obstinacy of him who persists in his own private way. This, however, cannot be regarded as an appropriate description of the spiritual situation of the Protestant Christian. In the course of a now centuries-old history, Protestantism has made an important contribution to the realization of Christian faith, fulfilling a positive function in the development of the Christian message and, above all, often giving rise in the individual non-Catholic Christian to a sincere and profound faith whose separation from the Catholic affirmation has nothing to do with the *pertinacia* characteristic of heresy. Perhaps we may here invert a saying of St. Augustine's which says that an old schism becomes a heresy. The very passage of time alters the character of a division, so that an old division is something essentially different from a new one. Something that was once rightly condemned as heresy cannot later simply become true, but it can gradually develop its own positive ecclesial nature which the individual is presented with as his church, and in which he lives as a believer, not as a heretic. This orginization of one group, however, ultimately has an effect on the whole. The conclusion is inescapable, then: Protestantism today is something different from heresy in the traditional sense, a phenomenon whose true theological place has not yet been determined. And here resides the whole difficulty of the question we have asked. A phenomenon of this kind simply does not arise anywhere in the New Testament or in the Fathers; hence we have no direct guidance in them as to how we are to regard the separated Christians of today. Rather must we try to think our way forward here in the spirit of the New Testament and to apply this spirit to all the things that did not exist then, but are in our world today. Such an attempt, which can be only barely outlined here and would need a lot of detailed preliminary study, would have to start from the recognition that in the mutual relationship of separated Christians there are two levels which must be carefully distinguished: the dogmatic one, and the concrete moral one. The answer differs according to the level about which we are speaking.

(a) The dogmatic position is that the objective presentation of the vicarious saving act of Jesus Christ can be performed by the one Church only, that is (according to Catholic belief), the Catholic Church which is gathered around the successor of Peter. We come here to the basic ecclesiological category (whose importance is only now beginning to be recognized) of *re-praesentatio*. Just as it is the essential nature of the sacraments to show forth by signs the hidden mystery of God, to proclaim publicly in the visible world the share of God in the drama of history, to witness to the invisible deity in the world of the visible, so it is with the great total sacrament that is the Church itself: it is the sign of God in the world, and its task is the visible and public witness to the divine saving will before the face of history. Although it serves the realizing of grace, it cannot be simply identified with grace. There is a difference between the symbolic presentation of the new order of grace before the world and the presence or absence of grace in a man's soul, which leads us into the hidden secrets of the human heart which no one but God can know. There is grace outside the sacraments and outside the visible Church: the dialogue of God with man is conducted by him in total freedom; but there is not some indeterminate number of churches or sacraments, but only the one sign of God through which he shows his mystery to the world. Once we see that the nature of the Church's existence is *re-praesentatio*—the public presentation of the saving reality of God—then it is obvious that there can be only one such valid sign. That does not mean that only Catholics make a positive contribution to the realizing of salvation, that only Catholics represent with Christ, while all others are merely represented and thus are only the negative shadow of Catholics. There is, rather, among individuals a great and interwoven pattern: what happens in the invisible order of grace is known ultimately to God alone who calls everyone by his name, which he alone knows who receives it (*cf.* Rev 2:17). It is the objective presentation of this vicarious work of Christ that it is reserved for the one Church which, because of this continuation of the saving act of the Lord, can alone be called the "true" Church.

(b) If we move now from the level of dogma to that of concrete human relationships, we can see from what we have said that the immediate brotherly community is made up of the communicants. Hence all those who are separated from the communion, in this case Protestants, do not belong to it. They have their own brotherhood, their own community. This is the nature of the divisions in the Church; some are no longer in communion with others, and thus sharing in the brotherhood of the Church (which was to be only one, according to the will of the Lord) is made impossible. And so, if the immediate narrow fraternal community is made up only of the believers of the one Church, we can ask at least that the two communities—Catholic and Protestant—regard each other as "sisters in the Lord." This is an idea which goes beyond Scripture and the Fathers (here, as we have seen, there is only the sisterliness of the Catholic communities), but which seems justified by the new situation of separated Christians. Both communities, as bearers of faith in an unbelieving world, can and should regard themselves as sisters, and individual Christians on both sides are "brothers" to each other in a far more fundamental sense than are non-Christians. Admittedly, this brotherhood between Catholics and Protestants includes the fact that both belong to a different fraternal community—includes, too, the separation, and the pain of this separation, and thus presents a constant challenge to overcome it. Indeed, it is important not to ignore the element of separation which is inevitably part of this brotherhood and gives it its particular quality: to ignore it is ultimately to become reconciled to it, and that is just what we must not do. "Separated brethren," which has become such a glib phrase, can thus acquire an exact and valuable meaning. It expresses the unity that remains as well as the tragedy of division. Thus the word should be a comfort, and also a spur—a spur that does not let us rest until there is "one flock, one shepherd" (Jn 10:16).